BEADING *with*
PEYOTE STITCH

Jeannette Cook
and *Vicki Star*

A BEADWORK
HOW-TO BOOK

INTERWEAVE PRESS

Editor, Judith Durant
Illustrations, Jason Reid
Production, Dean Howes
Cover design, Bren Frisch

Cover: *Tapestry Patchwork Collage Vessel* by Jeannette Cook. Photograph by Jeff Tippett.

Beadwork Magazine
Interweave Press
201 East Fourth Street
Loveland, Colorado 80537-5655
USA

Printed in the United States by Vision Graphics

Library of Congress Cataloging-in-Publication Data
Cook, Jeannette, 1954–
     Beading with peyote stitch/Jeannette Cook and Vicki Star.
          p. cm.
     Includes bibliographical references and index.
     ISBN 1-883010-71-3
     1. Beadwork. I. Star, Vicki, 1955– II. Title.
TT860.C6626 2000
746.5—dc21   00-025771

First printing: IWP-7.5M:300:VG

Table of Contents

Acknowledgements

*This book is dedicated to our
grandchildren–Chloé, Rita, and Josiah Nilles,
and Malcolm, Tabitha, and Diego Stumpf.
We love you!*

We extend a big "Thank You!" to all the fabulous beady staff at Interweave Press. And especially to our editor, Judith Durant, for making us sound so professional.

Thank you to everyone that took the time to send in pictures. It was really hard to choose from all that fabulous beadwork.

We'd also like to say thanks to Laura Breisacher for reccommending us, to Diane Fitzgerald for her help, to Joyce Scott for that first Sculptural Peyote lesson, and to all the students we've worked with throughout the years. You taught us how to teach, and we learned valuable lessons from you.

Jeannette would also like to thank her husband David. "He was sent to me to teach me patience. I haven't graduated yet. It is the hardest lesson I have to learn."

Introduction

Here we are, embarking on yet another book-writing adventure. We've already written six how-to beading books under the imprint of Beady Eyed Women's® Guides to Exquisite Beadwork. Two of these books are on peyote stitch. So why should we want to write another one?

Lots of reasons! We've learned a lot more about this technique in the three and a half years since we wrote our last book on peyote stitch. Much of this knowledge has come from teaching all across the country. Students continue to teach *us* more and more with each class. And the more we work with this amazing stitch, the more ideas we have. New uses for peyote stitch just keep popping into our heads. We often call each other and say, "Ooh, ooh! Wait till I show you what I'm working on now!"

Another reason is that we *like* writing these beading books. It's rewarding and uplifting when beaders tell us we have inspired them. And thanks to Interweave Press, a longtime dream of ours

Spirit Bead Legend

Muslim people believe that only Allah is perfect; therefore anything made by man should be imperfect not to offend Allah and bring bad luck. Native Americans believe that there must be a mistake in handwork to leave a pathway for the spirit, otherwise it may become trapped in the work. So don't panic if you spot a "wrong bead" in your work. Let it be your own personal spirit bead leading you on to new levels of creativity!

The Beader's Credo

I will learn as many techniques as I can.
I will share techniques with others.
I will follow the copyright laws.
I will give credit where credit is due.
I will support my local bead society.
I will accumulate as many beads as I can, while still paying my bills.

comes true: *color photos!* Wahoo! Lots of these photos illustrate peyote-stitch techniques. And there's a fabulous gallery of contemporary work by our students and other beady eyed friends.

As with any other art form, perfecting your technique sets you free to design. So bead, bead, bead. If something doesn't come out quite the way you wanted, figure out why. Try it another way. Maybe you can use your "practice piece," or what you learned from it, for the next project. There are no mistakes in beadwork, only opportunities for learning.

So we hereby officially give you permission to bead, and to make mistakes, and to have fun! We're going to start with the simplest, most basic form of peyote stitch, then move on to the more complex (and fun) versions. We'll share what we've learned, and we hope we inspire you to try something new.

Happy Beading,
Jeannette Cook & Vicki Star
The Original Beady Eyed Women

Some Peyote Stitch Background

*T*his particular beadwork technique has been around for a long, long time. Adding one bead at a time, the stitch produces a fabric of beads arranged like brick paving, one bead up and one bead down, in columns. Variations include two-drop, three-drop, and sculptural freeform.

There are several names for the technique: peyote stitch, twill stitch, diagonal weave, and gourd stitch; however, we haven't heard the terms twill stitch or diagonal weave used by any of our contemporaries. The term gourd stitch is used by Native American beadworkers and describes a specific use for peyote stitch. According to David Dean in his article "Is it Peyote or Beadweaving?" for *Beadwork* magazine (Summer/1999), gourd stitch is used by the Tiah Pia (Kiowa) to cover items such as the rattles and fans used in their gourd dances. Peyote stitch is used to describe beadwork done for ceremonial and religious purposes within the Native American Church. Purely for practical purposes, and without disrespecting Native American beadworkers, most contemporary beadworkers use the term peyote stitch simply to describe the technique, with no religious or cultural association.

The History of Beads by Lois Sherr Dubin features a photograph of a winged scarab done in what looks like two-drop peyote stitch. The piece dates to Old Kingdom Egypt, 2686–2181 B.C., and it makes us—and, indeed, many historians—wonder about the path this stitch has taken through time, becoming part of Native American and West African cultures, appearing in Victorian England, and now gaining so much favor with contemporary artisans.

Dubin tells us that beads were manufactured extensively in Egypt for commercial use about 1400 B.C. They were used every day, both men and women wore beaded items, and beads were among the treasures buried with the dead to ensure comfort in the afterworld. (Jeannette's trying to figure out who she'll be in the next life so she can leave her beads to herself!)

With the end of the nineteenth dynasty (c. 1200 B.C.), bead making skills declined, but were revived during the fourth century B.C. when Alexander the Great founded Alexandria, a city which developed international trading links. It's likely that Europeans got many of their beads through this Egyptian connection. Grave robbers would have sold their loot to the international traders, and craftspeople probably copied beading styles and techniques from these treasures.

Beaded Cache-sex. Three-mm tile beads, West Africa. Collection of Diane Fitzgerald.

A cache-sex is a beaded apron worn by women to cover the pubic area during dancing or festivities. With rhythmic movement, the cowrie shell fringe makes a delightful rustling sound. Made of 3-mm tile beads, the beadwork is supported by a heavy cotton cord that is tied around the waist in back. The diamond pattern in red, blue, white, and yellow is typical of this type of beadwork. The piece is 24" x 8" without the fringe. The strand for each vertical row of beads begins with a larkshead knot around the supporting cord, then the beads are woven together. Each pair of strands ends with a knot below the beadwork and another in the shell.

How Beads are Made

In the "olden days," artisans made seed beads by blowing a bubble of molten glass. Then an apprentice attached a "punty" or metal rod to the opposite side of the bubble and ran across the room, stretching the bubble into a long, skinny tube. This tube was then cut into individual beads, which were tumbled in hot sand to round the edges. The finished beads were sifted through different-sized screens for sorting. Artifacts from this method of bead making have been dated to 600–650 A.D.

Today, machines do most of the work, but stringing the beads into hanks is still a cottage industry in some countries. Women sit with several threaded needles in their hands and scoop through a bowl of beads to string them into hanks.

You can buy beads in hanks, tubes, or other packages, and by kilo, gram, or ounce. Most seed beads come from Czechoslovakia, France, Japan, or Taiwan. Czech beads are usually sold in hanks, while French and Japanese beads are mostly sold loose. Keeping in mind that these distinctions are not always true (beads are sometimes repackaged), you can use packaging as a clue to country of origin when you're looking at older beads.

The History of Peyote Stitch Beadwork According to Jeannette

I'm neither historian nor scholar. In fact, I'd never really thought much about how peyote stitch came into being until we started working on this book. I've since done some checking around, and what impressed me the most is how little peyote stitch history is available. I'm just happy I learned it and can use it to create my artwork and teach others.

I was taught peyote stitch while shopping at a bead store here in San Diego. This was about 1974, and I was chatting with the owner. When I mentioned that I didn't know peyote stitch, a gentleman shopper overheard and offered to show me the stitch right then and there. I didn't use the stitch much right away because I was selling my bead embroidery work at the time.

Years later, I had the opportunity to take a two-day workshop with Joyce Scott. She was on the cutting edge of wild and sculptural peyote stitch, and I'd never seen anything done with beads like what Joyce was doing. She used her peyote-stitch beadwork to express her political and social views. Wow! I was a changed woman. I put down my bead embroidery and peyote stitched from that weekend on.

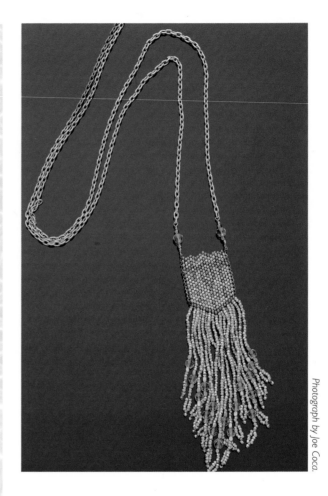

TinyPouch *with antique steel-cut beads. Beads circa 1920, French. Collection of Vicki Star.*

This tiny pouch was made using French steel-cut beads. The beads are actually steel, and they were available in silver, gold, brass, and a few other colors. They were usually woven on bead looms or knitted into purses. Nowadays, beadworkers who are lucky enough to find these purses, usually heavily damaged, cut them apart to reuse the beads. The beads for TinyPouch, however, were still on their original little "hanklets." An antique purse inspired the pouch's designs (the front and back are different). Since the finished TinyPouch is so heavy, Vicki used a sterling chain for the neck strap and reinforced the points of attachment with fine wire.

Modern Peyote Beadwork

Beadwork has come in and out of vogue through history. In the 1960s it was popular with hippies, but not taken seriously by the general public. Not until the early 1980s did beadwork become popular in America, and now it has snowballed into the huge resurgence we are currently experiencing.

Today beadwork is considered art in America, and peyote stitch is one of the most popular techniques employed. We think peyote is one of the most versatile methods known, and our contemporaries are doing amazing things with this stitch! Just look through the gallery on pages 67–109 to see the remarkable variety of art created with this basic stitch.

Photograph by Joe Coca.

Crystal with size 20° beads. Beads circa 1870, Czechoslovakian. Collection of Vicki Star.

Vicki worked this tubular peyote band with paisleys around the top of a blue lace agate crystal. It took about a half-hour for each row and there are thirty-one rows! The beads are tiny, and while there are even smaller ones out there, beads smaller than size 15° are getting hard to find.

The History of Peyote Stitch Beadwork According to Vicki

For me, beading is meditation. I love the rhythm and the feel of the beads in my hands. And, of course, the beads' sparkle and shine and color. I've been making things for as long as I can remember. I learned to crochet when I was four. My mom and my grandma and my sisters and I made headbands and belts out of yarn using finger crochet and chain stitch. I rapidly progressed to potholders and bedspreads for my dolls. I learned to loom-weave beads on a cigar box in Camp Fire Girls when I was eight. I strung love beads when I was in junior high school, and I have made my own jewelry for years. I'm lucky to have grown up in a crafty family.

I don't remember where I first learned peyote stitch, but it was probably from a book. I still have the first amulet purse I made, nearly fifteen years ago. I made a tube and sewed up the bottom, but I didn't like the way the bottom turned out. I fell asleep that night thinking of different ways to start and finish pouches. I woke up the next morning with an *Aha!* Now I start my pouches at the bottom, and there's no seam to sew up! And peyote stitch is still my favorite beading stitch.

Supplies

Wow! Beads! They're so beautiful, so tiny, so sparkly, so wonderful to hold! As our beady friend Cynthia Rutledge says, "There is no bead we do not need!"

We use mostly seed beads for peyote stitch. Seed beads come in a plethora of shapes, sizes, colors, and finishes. Colors and finishes vary much as dye lots of yarn and fabric do—it's hard to find the exact same color again, so make sure you buy enough beads to finish your project. And when you see beads you like, buy them! You may never see *those* beads again. Buy as many beads as you can afford. (Who needs to eat, anyway?)

Bead Sizes

Seed beads range in size from 3° (called crow beads) to 24° (we call these bead pollen). The number refers to the number of beads that will fit into a given space. The larger the number, the more beads in that space, therefore the smaller the bead. The "°" is pronounced "oh" or "ought". Size 11° beads are probably the most common.

Some Japanese beads are sized by millimeters. A size 11° Japanese seed bead is sometimes called a 1.9 mm Japanese bead and is a tiny bit bigger than an 11° from Czechoslovakia

Photograph by Joe Coca.

or France. Bead sizes can be very misleading—an 11° bead made by one manufacturer may be very different from those made by another; shape and finish also affect size. Japanese beads in general have larger holes than Czech beads of comparable size.

Bead Shapes

Most seed beads are shaped like donuts or Cheerios. When viewed from the side, they are oval in shape. Some have round holes, some have square holes. Seed beads decorated by faceting are called "cut" beads. "Charlottes" are usually size 13° or 14° beads that are hand cut on one ("one-cuts") or two ("two-cuts") sides. A side that is ground flat reflects the light and makes the beads sparkle and flash like tiny mirrors. Beads that are faceted fairly evenly all around are called "three-cuts" and are usually size 9° or 12°. Because three-cuts vary in size, they are a little more difficult to use. But they're worth the trouble—they look like little gems.

Japanese Delica or Antique beads (Antique and Delica are brand names, not an indication of age) work great for peyote stitch. These are similar to seed beads but are shaped more like little tubes than donuts. When seen sideways, they look square, rather than oval. Because their holes are larger than comparably-sized seed beads, they are easy for beginners to use. And they fit together very evenly, producing a stiffer fabric than rounded seed beads do.

There are also many novelty beads that are fun and beautiful. Try 4 mm cubes or triangle beads in 10°, 8°, or 5°. There are Magatamas and other teardrop shaped beads about the size of a 6° that create interesting effects. Nibblettes are flat brick-shaped beads with holes going lengthwise.

Bead Color

There are three basic types of bead colors. *Transparent* beads are those you can see through. *Translucent* beads have a chemical added to the molten glass to make them milky. *Opaque* beads do not transmit any light at all.

However, all beads reflect light and will affect the colors around them. Sometimes this feature results in happy surprises, sometimes unhappy ones. We recommend that you make a few sample squares before you start a project to see how your colors interact. A good book on color theory can also be very helpful.

Be aware that some beads, such as painted, dyed, and galvanized beads, will fade with time, exposure to light, and use. We try to avoid them. While the initial colors are so beautiful you will be tempted, you will be terribly disappointed when those beautiful purple metallic beads turn an ugly yellow-green about the third time you wear your new necklace. You can try to keep the finish of such beads from rubbing off by spraying them with a clear fixative like Krylon, but the fixative won't prevent fading. Ask at the store where you buy your beads if they are likely to change color. And you'll know for sure if your fingers and thread change to the same color as the beads while you work.

Bead Finishes

Luster is a shiny finish. Opaque luster beads are often called pearl, and opal luster beads are sometimes called Ceylon. A clear rainbow-like finish is called *AB* (Aurora Borealis). *Iris* beads are opaque, iridescent metallic-looking beads, usually in the purple, blue, brown, and green ranges. *Metallic* beads come in shades of bronze, copper, gunmetal, gold, or silver. These finishes hold up well. *Galvanized* beads tend to lose their finish and fade, so try to avoid them.

Lined beads

Silver lined beads with square holes are called "rocailles," although the Czechs often use this term for any seed bead. The silver used in rocailles will tarnish or darken with age like an old mirror.

Beads of one color may be lined with another color, such as yellow lined with pink, or lavender lined with blue. Watch out for faders here, too, because some beads are merely painted inside the holes instead of actually lined with a different color of glass. Translucent beads lined with white are called "white hearts." Their exteriors are usually red (called "Cornaline D'Aleppo"), although we've also seen them in pink, blue, orange, yellow, and turquoise. The white lining makes them seem to light up.

Other finishes

Some seed beads are striped, with the stripes running lengthwise, parallel to the hole. *Satins* are striated beads that shine like a tiger eye or star sapphire. Some white satins look like little mother-of-pearl beads. Beads may also be etched in acid to produce soft lustrous matte or semi-matte finishes.

Other Beads

Bugles are long thin tubes of glass. They range in length from 2 to 35 mm. Their ends can be very sharp, so be careful not to cut your thread or your fingers. Some people file the ends with emery paper to smooth them. (Bugles with a matte finish are not as sharp.) With peyote stitch, you can combine bugles with an equal length of seed beads for an interesting effect.

The variety of "other" beads is endless. Wood, glass, stone, and plastic are but a few of the materials used to make beads. Two to six millimeters are appropriate sizes for peyote-stitch beads, but you can also stitch around, over, or through large accent beads.

Culling Your Beads

If you are doing flat peyote stitch, and you want the beadwork to *be* flat, you must use beads that are all the same size. Uniform bead size is a mark of professional quality beadwork. To check for equal sizing between different types of beads, put several of each type on your needle. This makes it easy to compare sizes.

As you work, you will probably run into beads with odd shapes and sizes. They may be fat or skinny, crooked, or have an off-center hole. If a bead is really crooked or damaged, throw it away. (Fling it over your shoulder for good luck!) Save the too-fat and too-skinny beads for increasing and decreasing, or for use in another project. Odd-sized beads are great for sculptural peyote.

Avoid beads whose holes are smaller than the rest. If the bead is tight on the needle the first time you go through it, don't use it—you will have to go through it again at some point, and you may break the bead, the needle, or the thread in attempting to pass through. If many of your beads are tight, switch to the next smaller needle and/or thread size.

Storage

Students are always asking us how we keep our beads neat and tidy. The following are some of our favorite storage options.

Plastic bags

Small plastic zipper bags make it easy to see the bead color while they keep the beads clean and dust free. Plastic bags are also easy to transport, but they tend to discolor and split over time.

Plastic boxes

Plastic segmented boxes like those sold in craft stores are another option. These are easy to carry around, but difficult to work out of. Re-arranging your beads in the compartments can be difficult. And if the dividers are movable, beads tend to pass underneath from one compartment to the next. You may keep seed beads in zipper bags or on their hanks to minimize unwanted bead mixtures.

Toolboxes

A medium sized fishing tackle, toolbox, or artist's tackle box is a good place to store all your supplies and keep them ready for transport. The different-sized compartments hold beads, needles, scissors, and so on. They're made to be hard to tip over. When closed, they are "watertight": If they do tip over, the fishing lures, tools, or in our case beads and findings, don't spill or get mixed up. When the boxes open, everything is organized and easy to reach.

Parts cabinets

We use parts cabinets with different-size drawers, but they are not easy to move. (It's a real tragedy if they tip over in your car, especially if your beads are loose!) The clear drawers allow you to see what's inside.

We keep most of our beads in these. One cabinet is for size 11° seeds, one for delicas, one for semiprecious, one for fringe beads; you get the idea. We keep our beads by color, making it easy to pull out drawers for a project. Most beads are in zipper bags or tubes, or on strands inside the drawers. You can pull out all the drawers and rearrange them fairly easily to make room for new colors.

Containers

Most beaders we know love to save things like breath-mint boxes, film cans, pill bottles, plastic tubes, and baby food and bait jars to hold their beads. There are many plastic keepsake boxes available. Fishing tackle stores have some ingenious hook and bait boxes. Friends are always showing us nifty boxes they have found, originally made for any number of purposes.

Work Surfaces

A good work surface is easy to pick up beads from while keeping them from rolling around the room. Here are several options.

Leather

Leather or ultrasuede makes a perfect surface to bead from. Either one keeps the beads from rolling around too much and provides a convenient place to stick your needle between beading sessions. Line a tray or plate (something with a raised edge to help prevent spills) with leather or ultrasuede in a light neutral color.

Cloth

Many types of cloth also make a good work surface. Vicki likes to work on a flat white tea towel. It has enough texture to keep the beads from rolling around, but not enough for them to get lost in. Fold a towel to fit in a wooden serving tray and keep each project in a separate tray. That way they can be moved off the kitchen table when it's time for dinner. Velvet or other short-napped fabrics work well, too.

Terrycloth toweling doesn't work well—the pile is too deep and the beads get lost. Plus your needle can catch the loops. And stay away from felt; it sheds little thread fibers into your beadwork. A paper towel will work if you run out of tea towels or forget to bring your cloth to class.

Chrysanthemum dishes

Divided porcelain paint trays keep your beads separated while you work, but we find them too slippery as they come from the store; the beads slide around on the porcelain instead of jumping onto the needle. To solve this, line each section with ultrasuede (a light color for most beads, a few sections with a dark color for pale beads).

These dishes fit nicely, two to a case, in plastic pistol cases. Pistol cases are available in the hunting sections of your local Kmart or Wal-Mart. If you turn the bumpy foam pieces over

to their smooth sides, your beads can't spill when the case is closed; this feature makes the cases mighty handy for taking projects on the road. (Thanks to Virginia Blakelock for figuring this out and sharing it with all of us!)

Findings

Findings are the parts you may need to finish your work, especially jewelry. You will need ear wires, clips, or posts of some type to put the finishing touch on earrings. You may need some type of clasp to finish a bracelet or a necklace. You may also need barrette or pin backs.

You can buy ready-made findings or make your own. A beautiful button and a reinforced loop of seed beads makes a perfect clasp for many bracelets or necklaces. Or use 16 or 18 gauge wire to bend a hook and eye closure. Use 20 gauge gold-filled, sterling, or niobium wire to make your own ear wires.

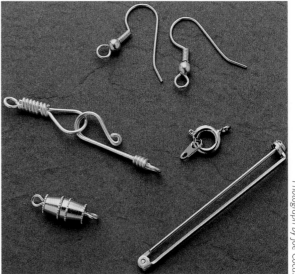

Photograph by Joe Coca.

Don't skimp on the quality here. Once you've put all that work into your project, you should use the very best findings that complement and enhance your beadwork. One of our pet peeves comes from a beader putting many hours and lots of expensive beads into a necklace, and then using a fifty-cent clasp! Don't do it! Your time and skill are worth more (way more) than that!

Needles, Thread, and Wax

Needles

Beading needles are long and thin. Because the eyes are much smaller than those on sewing needles, they fit through the tiny hole in small beads.

Long needles work well when you need to pick up several beads at once, for example when stringing fringes. Short "sharps" needles are only about one inch long and are good for peyote stitch. Since you are picking up only one bead at a time, you don't need the length of a regular beading needle. Sharps are also good for working in tight places, such as small amulet bags or vessels. Sharps needles are strong, and they won't break, as the longer needles do, when you're sewing your beadwork to leather.

The smallest beading needle we have is a size 16, the largest is a size 10. Size 10 or 12 sharps work well with size 11° seed beads or delicas. Use a 13 or 15 beading needle with size 14° seeds, and a 16 needle with size 20° beads. Needles from different manufacturers,

Photograph by Joe Coca.

and sometimes needles in a packet of the same size, are subtly different. Some have larger eyes or are slightly thinner or longer than the next. Experiment with different brands until you find your favorite.

Handle your needles with care. Longer needles tend to become curved as you work. To help prevent this, pull each stitch tight by yanking on the thread, not the needle. When a needle gets too curly to control, throw it away. Stick curved or broken needles through a heavy piece of paper and fold it over so no one will get hurt taking out the trash. On the other hand, you may want to keep a few broken needles (the short part with the eye still intact) to use when tying off that last tiny end of thread that you knew you should have tied off in the last row. (But you only had a few more beads to go!)

Thread

Here are a few things to consider when choosing the thread for your project.

Thread color

Thread will show through transparent and translucent beads, so it will change the color of the bead. This feature can add a subtle glow to your work or create a garish effect, so choose your thread colors carefully. If you're using white thread, and any thread shows through where it shouldn't, you can color it with a permanent marker that matches your beads. Some people like to use black thread, because they feel it makes the bead colors look brighter.

Thread types

There are several brands and types of beading thread. Nymo and Silamide are our favorites for peyote stitch. They are both easy to find and hold up well.

Nymo beading thread is the most popular. Nymo stands for *nylon monofilament*, and its fibers run straight, like dental floss. It comes in sizes OOO, OO, O, A, B, C, D, E, F and G; OOO is the thinnest and G is the heaviest. As a general rule, size B thread works well with 11° beads. Size D is good with delicas. (Please feel free to break the rules!)

Silamide is a twisted nylon thread used by tailors. Size A works well for most beadwork. Since it's thicker than Nymo, and twisted, it's a little harder to thread into a needle. It's pre-waxed, but it's easier to use if you wax it again (see below). It's also a little more slippery than Nymo, especially if you don't rewax it.

Beading thread is really strong. When it breaks in the middle of a row (and it will!) it's usually because a bead with a sharp spot cuts it. Watch for frays, and start a new thread if you notice any.

Threading a Needle

Because the eyes of beading needles are so small, threaders don't usually work. They tend to weaken the needle eye so much (if you can even get the threader in) that the eye will break as soon as you put any pressure on it.

To thread your needle, first make sure you have plenty of light. Hold your needle over something white so you can see through the eye. Cut the thread end at a sharp, clean angle. Bite the end between your front teeth to flatten it, moisten the end, or lightly wax it. Moisten the *eye* of the needle. Pinch the thread between your thumb and index finger with just the teensiest bit sticking out, and put the needle on the thread.

Threading your needle is half the battle. If you have trouble, you can always get beady eyed friends to thread up a whole pack of needles for you. (You may have to bribe them with a bead or two.)

For most projects, thread your needle with about two yards of thread. To keep the thread from becoming tangled, thread the end that comes off the spool, then measure out the two yards and snip. Don't make your thread so long that you must keep pulling and pulling it through the beads—you'll end up with a tired arm and lots of tangles, and the thread will wear and weaken.

Wax

Coating your thread with wax will help keep it from tangling or fraying, make it slide through the beads more easily, and strengthen it. We like the micro-crystalline wax because it's softer and stickier than beeswax.

Thread Heaven is a realtively new product that provides a Teflon coating for your thread. It helps prevent tangles, and some of our students love it. But we prefer wax because it's easier to control the tension of sticky waxed thread than slippery Thread Heaven-coated thread.

Waxing your thread

After you thread your needle, hold the thread below the eye. Now press the thread against the wax with your other thumb, and pull. Repeat two or three times along the length of the thread. Run your fingers along the thread to remove any excess or you'll end up with little globs of wax between your beads. If this happens, use a soft cloth and a little friction to "polish" the excess wax away. A soft toothbrush works really well, too.

Other Tools

Scissors

A small pair of sharp scissors or snippers is essential. It is much easier to thread your needle if your thread is smoothly cut and no frays stick out to foil your efforts. You also need to be able to cut off your thread tails close to your work.

Pliers

A pair of chain nose pliers can break away an extra bead. To do this, place the tips of your pliers across the bead from hole to hole, then squeeze gently. Don't smash the bead onto the thread, and be careful not to cut yourself or the thread. Be extra careful not to get bits of glass in your eye.

Pliers can also help coax your needle and thread through a tight spot. Grab the needle as close to the bead as you can with the wider part of the jaws, and gently twist and wiggle it on through.

Needle grabber

Use a wide rubber band or circular piece of rubber (cut from an old rubber glove, or buy one at a sewing store) to grab your needle and help coax it through a snug spot.

Glue

E-6000, a clear silicone glue, is great for attaching findings such as earring posts and pin backs to your beadwork. Barge All-Purpose Cement and E-6000 work well for attaching a leather backing to a cabochon that you want to bead around. Make sure that all parts are clean before gluing. Wax, dirt, or oil from your hands will cause a poor bond.

Use clear nail polish or G S Hypo Tube Cement to seal knots. Be careful not to use too much!

Light

Light is one of the most important components of your beadwork. Good light makes working with tiny beads much, much easier. Be kind to your eyes. Several types of lamps are available. Halogen bulbs give a good, strong light. Fluorescent bulbs will distort the color of your beads as will incandescent bulbs; if you use either sort of bulb, look at your beads in daylight to decide on color combinations. Full spectrum bulbs simulate natural sunlight and are best for your eyes and your beads. Ott is one brand of full spectrum lamp and light bulb that is wonderful for beading and other arts. Some lamps even come with magnifying lenses built right in.

It is also very important to rest your eyes every fifteen to twenty minutes. To change the focus of your eyes and give them a break from the close work they've been doing, look out a window. Look as far away as possible. While you're at it, roll your shoulders, shake out your hands and arms, and relax your neck muscles. Beading is much more fun when you're not in pain!

Fire

We each carry a small lighter in our beading kits because the flame is helpful for melting off fuzzy thread ends and sealing knots. Trim off the thread as close to your work as you can. If any thread is sticking out, bring it close to the flame; the thread will shrivel up and disappear. Try this on a scrap of thread first to see how it works. Don't burn yourself! You can also use matches or a candle.

Fire cleans out the eye of a needle that is clogged with wax. Pass the eye quickly through the flame. You may see a tiny puff of black smoke. Polish the needle with a soft cloth to remove any soot.

Graph paper and patterns

Complex patterns require planning and graphing on special peyote graph paper with erasable colored pencils. There are numerous patterns and graph papers available. If you have a transparency of your graph paper made at your local copy shop, you can lay it over a picture or design. Voila! You have an instant pattern!

There is also some great beading software available for your computer. These programs are terrific timesavers over the old-fashioned paper and pencil method. See the source list on page 110 for paper and programs.

Rulers

You can custom-make a ruler to help you follow your pattern. Use a piece of clear plastic from a report cover or transparency sheet; cut it about an inch wide and as long as your pattern is wide. Lay it horizontally on your pattern, and trace around the first row of beads with a black permanent fine-tipped pen. Outline the second row with another color. Now line up the black outlines with the row you're on, and the colored outline will be the row to do next.

Other Objects

You may want to cover or decorate an object with peyote stitch. Suitable items include (but please don't limit yourself to) small perfume bottles or pill containers, crystals, lighters, pens, gourds, dowels, feathers, wooden beads, pieces of driftwood, rocks, rolled scraps of leather, or shapes made from wire, cloth, or polymer clay.

O

Okay, got everything ready?

You have a comfortable chair, a good light, and an ample supply of beads. Your needle is threaded and waxed. All right then. Let's bead!

Techniques

First let's talk a little about your options regarding thread and knots. Should you use a single or double thread? Should you tie knots? What size thread should you use? Well, it depends.

Single Versus Doubled Thread

The thread you choose has to fit through your beads. A thin, single thread will produce a flexible, soft, piece that lies flat like fabric. For a stiff, freestanding piece, use thick and/or doubled thread. The heavier the thread, the stiffer the piece.

Flexible work with single thread

Vicki uses a single thread on her patterned beadwork. The smaller the holes in the beads, the thinner the thread must be. When you're using a single thread, pull the needle about two-thirds of the way along the length of thread. As you use up the working thread, slide the needle farther along the "tail" to give you more thread to work with. With a single thread you don't have to thread the needle as often, and if you need to do the "frog stitch" (that's when you have to rip it! rip it!), you can simply unthread the needle and pull the thread out of your work back to a point before the mistake. To keep the piece flexible, don't pull the thread too tightly as you work; keep the tension loose.

Self-Supporting work with doubled thread

Jeannette likes a doubled thread for her sculptural peyote work. The larger the holes in the beads, the thicker the thread must be. For a stiff, freestanding piece, use thick and/or doubled thread, pass through the holes often, and keep the tension tight as you work. The more you fill the holes with thread, the stiffer the piece will be.

If you need to undo a portion of your work, just pull the needle, eye first, backwards through the beads. Never try to undo your work by putting the needle point-first back through the beads—you'll end up tying knots and splitting the thread and making an even bigger mess. So don't do it! And if you do, don't say we didn't warn you!

Starting Your Beadwork

A "keeper" or "stopper" bead prevents the working beads from escaping off the tail of your thread when you're beginning your beadwork. Tie a keeper bead loosely onto the end of your thread, leaving a six-inch tail to weave into the work later. (This bead will be removed before you weave in the tail, so don't count it when counting beads in the first row.)

When you reach the end of the third row, both the tail and the needle threads should be coming out of the same bead (on even-number peyote) or from two adjacent beads (on odd-number peyote). At this point you have two choices. You may tie a knot and cut off the tail thread now, or leave it alone and weave it in later.

Knotting the starting thread

Remove the keeper bead, tie your two threads together in a square knot, and put a drop of glue or nail polish on the knot. Cut off the tail thread and continue beading.

Weaving in the starting thread

If you don't begin your beadwork by knotting the starting thread, you may use this thread as a "handle" while starting. You can also easily add other thread and beads without running into a knot. When you are ready to weave in the starting thread, remove the keeper bead and thread the tail onto a needle. Zigzag the thread through the beadwork (see page 22), reversing directions several times, and trim off any remaining thread.

Adding new thread

For most beadwork, it's impossible to use a thread long enough to finish the whole piece. So when you're down to the last four to six inches of thread, you need a way to tie off and add new thread. It's usually easier if you stop in the middle of a row. Be sure to allow enough thread with which to tie off or weave in, no matter how tempting it is to do "just a few more beads!"

If you have a large area of beadwork, you can finish off with no knots. But if your piece is very small or you need extra stiffness, you may tie several knots before ending your thread. Be careful not to pull too tightly when ending or beginning new threads—this could create unwanted ripples in your beadwork.

The no-knot jig

We've been using and teaching this method for years, and it's just as secure as knotting. One advantage is that there are no knots to run into later. And sometimes, if your bead-work is tight, it's impossible to tie knots be-cause you can't work in between the beads. It can also be difficult to hide knots.

When you're four to six inches from the end of your thread, head diagonally down through several beads. Bring the thread out and go through the bead directly above the one you just came out of. Now head diago-nally down in the opposite direction.

Making these little Xs by changing the direc-tion of the thread really anchors it in place. Try to change direction at least three times. If any thread shows, you've skipped a bead—carefully pull the thread out and try again. When you're happy with the jig, cut off the end as close to the beadwork as possible.

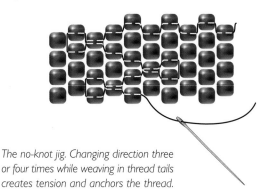

The no-knot jig. Changing direction three or four times while weaving in thread tails creates tension and anchors the thread.

Start a new thread by sewing in a zigzag pattern through beads a few rows below where you want the thread to emerge. Leave a few inches of thread, hold on to this tail so you don't pull the thread through, and work up the same way, jigging and jogging to come out where you left off, ready to continue beading. You can find this spot by looking for the place where three beads "stairstep." You want to come out the middle bead, heading towards the lowest "step." (See the star in the drawing.)

Add a new thread with the no-knot jig, ending where you left off with the old thread.

Adding thread with knots

When you're four to six inches from the end of your thread, *run your needle diagonally down and to the left, through several beads. Come out on the wrong, or back, side of your work. Tie a knot around the core thread by bringing your needle from the back to the front and then from the front to the back, just below and to the left of the same bead. Leave a small loop of thread on the wrong

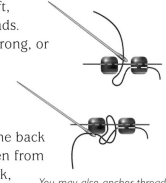

You may also anchor thread tails by knotting around the core thread.

side. Put your needle through the loop from right to left, and pull everything up tight. Be sure the knot tightens *between* the beads.

Repeat from * at least once more. Cut the thread off as close to the work as possible.

Start a new thread by passing through beads a few rows below where you want the thread to emerge. Make a knot around the core thread as described above. Work your way up diagonally toward the bead where you left off, tying at least one more knot on the way up. Come out through the bead where you left off, ready to continue beading.

Finishing

Finish off the last thread of your work with the same method you used to finish off old threads (with or without knots), but here you'll have to finish off at the end of the final row, rather than in the middle. Trim off tail threads and singe any fuzzies.

Basic Even-Number Flat Peyote

This method calls for one size of seed bead, and you may use it to create squares for earrings or a brooch, or to make a long, narrow strip for a neck chain. A one-by-seven-inch rectangle made with flat peyote makes a great bracelet. Sew six squares together for a box or connect two large rectangles for a purse.

Begin by putting a keeper bead on your thread (see Starting your beadwork on page 20). If you're new to beading, try using cubes or 6° beads. These large beads make it easier to see what you're doing.

To create a flat rectangle of beadwork that is an even number of beads wide, string an odd number of beads on your thread. For example, for a piece that is twelve beads wide, start with thirteen beads. These beads count as the first two rows. We suggest trying thirteen to nineteen beads to start.

Move the beads to within a few inches of the keeper bead on the tail of your thread. Put your needle through the third bead from the needle, marked with a star in Figure 1.

Holding on to the bead you're passing through with one hand, use the other hand to pull the thread all the way through. The first bead will sit on top of the second bead. (You may need to coax it into position.) See Figure 2.

Pick up a new bead with the needle and pass through the fifth bead from the beginning. Pick up another bead and pass

through the seventh bead (Figure 3). Continue in this manner, picking up a bead and passing through every other bead, to the end of this *third* row.

Both the tail and the needle threads will be coming out of the last bead (Figure 4).

Figure 1. *To begin the third row, pass through the third bead from the needle.*

Figure 2. *The first bead sits on top of the second bead.*

Figure 3. **Pick up a new bead, skip a bead, pass through the next bead; repeat from * to the end of the third row.*

Figure 4. *At the end of the third row, both the tail and working threads will come out of the same bead.*

To tighten your work, use your fingernails to push each set of two beads down away from the tail, and pull the two thread ends apart. At this point, Jeannette would tie the threads in three knots, put a dot of clear nail polish or glue on the knot, and continue beading. Vicki would just keep beading and weave the tail in later.

*Add a bead and pass through the second bead from the end (this is an "up" bead). **Add a bead and pass through the next "up" bead (Figure 5). Repeat from ** to the end of the row. Turn your beadwork over, and repeat from * until your piece is as tall (or long) as you want.

Figure 5. Once the third row is completed, you will have "up" beads to pass through for subsequent rows.

Basic Odd-Number Flat Peyote

If you want to bead a design with a centerline, you'll need to use this method. It is worked basically the same as even-number peyote stitch, except that on one edge of the work you'll have to make a different kind of turn, and anchor your thread a little differently.

Begin as for even-number peyote, but this time string on an *even* number of beads. (For example, use twelve beads to get a piece eleven beads wide.) When you've completed the third row (i.e., returned to the edge with the beginning bead), you will have one more bead on the tail thread. Add another bead to the needle thread and tie the two threads together with a square knot. Now pass back through the bead just added.

With odd-number peyote, you end the third row by knotting the working and tail threads together.

If you prefer not to have knots in your beadwork, use the following method. When you've completed the third row, turn and pass through the bead on the tail, then add a bead and continue. The next rows will hold the beads in place. *Note:* This method turns the first three rows upside-down. If you are following a pattern and the first and third rows are the same, proceed as usual. If the first and third rows are *not* the same, begin by stringing beads for the third and second row of your pattern, then work the first row. Now you may proceed as usual with the fourth row.

Continue as usual, adding one bead at a time and passing through the "up" beads across each row. From now on, one edge will be "normal" but the other edge will have no turn bead. When you're at the edge without the turn bead, catch the outside thread from the previous row to anchor the edge bead in place, then pass back through the same bead and continue the row.

You will end subsequent rows by looping the working thread through the thread from previous rows.

You may also run your thread through beads to anchor the edge bead, changing direction a couple of times as follows. Pass down through two beads, move up one bead, pass down through two beads in the opposite direction, move up and pass back through the edge bead.

Another way of ending rows is to pass back through the beadwork, changing direction a couple of times, and ending ready to begin the next row.

Photograph by Jeff Tippett

Jeannette made this Magic Carpet necklace with flat and tubular peyote stitch.

TipTipTip

Hold the needle in your dominant hand and the beads in the other. Don't try to work with the beadwork on the table—you'll just make it hard on yourself and **you'll end up with a sore neck. Wrap the tail of the thread loosely around the little finger of your non-dominant hand to help hold the beadwork and control the thread tension.**

A word or three about counting with peyote stitch. The beads you put on your thread at the beginning are actually for the first *and* second rows. When you go back along these beads to create the next row, the added beads become the *third* row. It is the third-row beads that pull and push the first- and second-row beads into place.

If you're doing freeform beadwork, you don't really have to think about this. But if you're following a pattern, then you need to pay attention, so your first-row beads stay on the bottom and your third-row beads stay on top.

In this illustration, the numbers are rows, the letters are columns. A bead can now be designated by its coordinates, so bead 3B is the bead in row 3, column B. Note that there is no bead 3A. Column A beads will be in even-numbered rows, column B beads will be in odd-numbered rows, and so on. When counting rows, whether on a pattern or on the beadwork, it's easiest to count them diagonally.

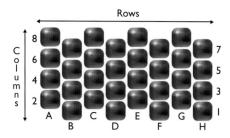

To make following (or creating) a pattern for flat peyote easier, think of the beads as residing in rows and columns.

Double-Bead Peyote

This is also called two-drop peyote, and by using a combination of bead sizes and shapes, or three or four or more bead sets (three-drop, four-drop, etc.), you can create a multitude of textural effects. You may also use double-bead peyote to make a transition to bugle or larger beads.

Put an even number of two-bead "sets" on the threaded needle. Treat each set of two beads as one unit. For help in seeing a pattern, alternate colors—two dark beads, two light beads, etc. (Figure 1).

Add two beads. Pass back through the second set from the beads you just added (Figure 2).

Add two beads and pass back through the fourth set. If you've used alternate light and dark beads, note that you will pass back through the same color you've just added. Continue in this manner across the row (Figure 3).

When you reach the end of the row, both the tail and the needle threads will come out of the same bead (Figure 4).

Add two beads and begin row four, working as described above. Continue until piece is desired size and finish off threads as described on pages 21 and 22.

Figure 1. For double-bead peyote, begin with an even number of two-bead sets.

Figure 2. Proceed as for single bead peyote, but add two beads, skip two beads, and pass back through the next two beads.

Figure 3. Continue working in sets of two across the row.

Figure 4. At the end of the third row, both the tail and working threads will come out of the same bead.

The Curl

This technique adds dimension to your work. Curls at the edge of your work can have larger beads nestled in them. If you make a big enough curl, it will look like an organic shell.

After you've done a few (between three and seven) rows of flat peyote stitch and you're at the end of a row, add two beads instead of one, then turn and pass back through the second (or "up") bead as usual, heading for the opposite side (Figure 1, below).

Figure 1. At the end of a row, add two beads instead of one.

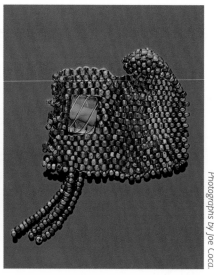

Jeannette used the curl to create a nest for a larger bead, while Vicki used it to shape the edge of her pin.

Bead normally to the opposite end, make the usual turn, and work back to the "two-bead" end. *Pass through the first of the two beads, add a bead, and pass through the second of the two beads (Figure 2).

You are not skipping any beads here. This is what increases the row and causes the beads to "tip" and begin to curl. Now, add two beads, turn, and pass back through the bead you just put between the previous two beads (Figure 3).

Work back to the other end, turn, and work back to the "two-bead" end. Repeat from * until you've completed the desired number of rows. The more rows, the bigger the curl!

Be sure you keep the tension tight at the two-bead end, allowing it to bend and curl. The biggest mistake we see in classes is smashing the curl flat. Let the end curl over your thumb while you tighten the stitches.

Figure 2. Add a bead between the two beads added at the end of the previous row.

Figure 3. Create the curl by again adding two beads at the end of the row instead of one.

Tubular Peyote

Tubular peyote is a variation of peyote stitch that forms a hollow, cylindrical shape. The tube may consist of an even or odd number of beads in each row, and you can use it to cover things such as crystals, dowels, bottles, and jars, to make hollow vessels, to bead bands for hats or wine glasses, or to create a "rope" of beads. A short tube makes a perfect nestlike setting for a larger bead. A small tube *is* a bead. A long skinny tube can be a bracelet; an even longer tube makes a necklace. If you make a really big tube, squash it flat, and sew up the bottom: it's a purse.

Tubular peyote is used extensively for making pictorial amulet bags. We've seen patterns of animals, nature, classic artwork, and even renditions of photographs of pets and kids. Anything you can scan or photocopy can be turned into a pattern for peyote stitch.

To begin, string the beads for your first and second rows. If the tube of beads is to fit on an object you're covering, you'll need enough beads to fit snugly around it but not so tight that you can't easily get your needle in and out of the beads. Now pass through all the beads again to form a circle. Pass through one more bead again (yes, this will be the third time through that bead), and the ring will hold its circular shape. Don't make this first row too tight: In order for the beads in subsequent rows to move into their up/down positions, you'll need a little slack in the thread. To maintain slack when you're begin-

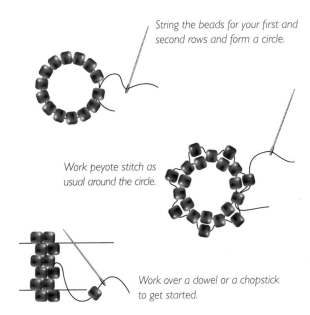

String the beads for your first and second rows and form a circle.

Work peyote stitch as usual around the circle.

Work over a dowel or a chopstick to get started.

ning your piece, try not to tie any knots until you've finished three or four rows.

The tube progresses from bottom to top. Once you've formed the circle, begin working the tube as follows. *String one bead on your needle, skip one bead of the core circle, and sew through the next bead of the core circle. Repeat from * until you get all the way around the circle.

When you're beading around an object, slide the core circle of beads onto the item before you begin to stitch. If you want to make a tiny tube that stands on its own, work over a dowel or chopstick to get started. Taping the tail thread to the item keeps the beadwork from sliding around. When you've finished the item, remove the tape and tie off the tail.

If you didn't count how many beads you have in the first two rows (and you probably didn't unless you are following a pattern), you'll now notice that one of two things will be required, depending on whether you have an even or odd number of beads. You're looking at the number of beads in two rows, or the number of columns (see page 26).

Even-Number Tubular Peyote

If you have an even number of beads, you'll have to step up through two beads to begin each row. Every row has a definite beginning and end.

Even-number peyote requires that you "step up" by passing through two beads at the end of the row—the last bead from the previous row and the first bead added in the current row.

Odd-Number Tubular Peyote

If you have an odd number of beads, you'll be able to just keep going, adding one bead at a time and passing through the next "up" bead. You are actually making one long row that spirals around and around. If you're beading a design with different colored beads, you'll have to pay attention to where each row starts so your pattern will be even.

For a spiral design, start by alternating two beads of each color, then make sure each bead you add in subsequent rows is the same color as the bead you just passed through. To reverse the spiral, add the same color bead as the one you will be passing through.

When working odd-number peyote, no step up is necessary.

Circular Peyote

Circular peyote stitch is a variation that produces a flat circle or disk of beadwork. Use this technique to cover the bottom of a bottle or the top of its lid, or to make the bottom of a bowl or vessel. Or use it simply to make a circle for any purpose.

To begin, string three to five beads, then pass through them again to make a ring. Pass through the first bead one more time (Figure 1). Leave a tail to tie off or weave in later.

Add one bead between each bead of the previous row (Figure 2). This is a regular row.

Finish each row by passing through the first bead of the previous row, then the first bead of the current row.

Add two beads between each bead of the second row (Figure 3). This is an increase row.

Continue alternating between increase and regular rows, depending on the degree of curve (or flatness) desired and the size of

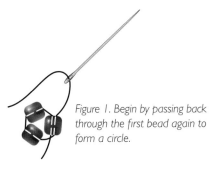

Figure 1. Begin by passing back through the first bead again to form a circle.

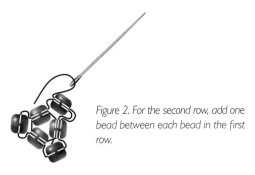

Figure 2. For the second row, add one bead between each bead in the first row.

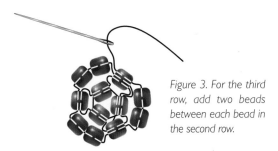

Figure 3. For the third row, add two beads between each bead in the second row.

your beads. If you increase a lot, the piece will begin to ruffle at the edges. If you increase only a little, the piece will begin to cup and form a bowl shape.

If you begin with circular peyote but then stop increasing, the form becomes tubular peyote. This is how you make a vessel or a bowl.

Shaping Your Beadwork

To add dimension to your peyote work, you may shape the edges or increase and decrease within the body of the work.

Shaping the Top and Bottom Edges

Zigzag edges

Begin with your thread coming out of an "up" bead. *Add one bead, pass through the next "up" bead, pass through the next "down" bead, pass through the next "up" bead, and repeat from *. Essentially you're adding a bead, passing through three beads, and adding the next bead.

You can create a zigzag edge by adding a bead between every other "set" of "up" beads.

Here's a pretty variation that takes two rows to complete. Begin with your thread coming out of an "up" bead.

Row 1: *Add one bead, pass through the next "up" bead, add one bead, pass through the next "up" bead, pass through the next "down" bead, pass through the next "up" bead. Repeat from *. You'll end up with sets of two "up" beads.

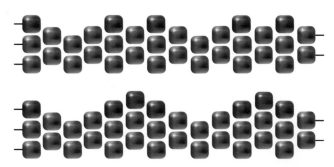

You may vary the zigzag edge by skipping more or fewer sets of up beads.

stitch all the way to the edge, including the three new beads as usual (Figure 3).

Begin each new stair step with the three beads (Figure 4).

You can begin a stair step with any odd number of beads. Just pass back through the third added bead, *add a bead, skip a bead, pass through the next bead. Repeat from * back to the main beadwork.

Row 2: Begin with your thread coming out of the first in a set of "up" beads. *Add one bead, pass through the next five beads. Repeat from *

Vary this zigzag as desired. The only limits are how many times you can fit your needle and thread through the "down" beads and the length of your beadwork's edge.

Shaping the Side Edges

For flat pieces that are irregularly shaped on one or both edges, use any or all of the following techniques.

Stair-step increasing

At the end of a row, add three beads and pass back through the first bead added (Figure 1).

Add a bead and sew through the first "up" bead in the original peyote-stitched area (Figure 2).

Continue working peyote stitch to the end of the row and back. On the return,

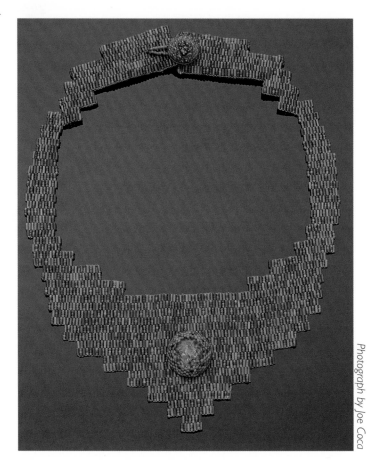

Springrtime Necklace *by Jolie Mann is a good example of stair-step increasing and decreasing.*

Stair-step increasing

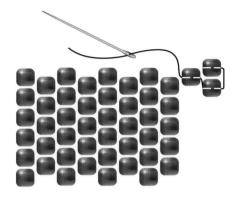

Figure 1. Add three beads for the first step of the increase.

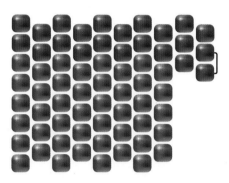

Figure 3. When you come back to the three increase beads, work them with peyote stitch as usual.

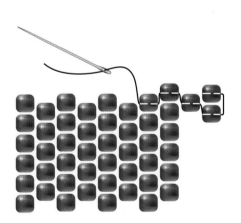

Figure 2. Add a new bead and continue as usual.

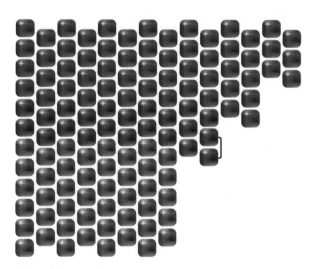

Figure 4. Begin each new stair as described above.

Stair-step decreasing

To decrease, you can simply turn back at any point in the row and work back to the opposite edge.

Depending on where you choose to turn back, you may have to anchor your thread as for odd-number peyote stitch. This is illustrated at right.

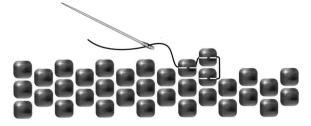

To decrease, simply stop the row short.

Decreasing at an angle

Use this technique on both edges when you want a triangle shape on the top (or bottom) of your beadwork.

When you reach an edge of your beadwork, pass through the loop between the two end beads. Pull the thread tight and pass back through the "down" bead and the next "up" bead. Notice that no bead was added.

To decrease at an angle, make a turn at the end of a row without adding a bead.

Continue to work peyote stitch across the row, decreasing at the opposite edge if desired, and back. When you reach the decreased edge, don't add a bead; just pass through the loop between the bead you are coming out of and the next bead down. Turn and pass through the bead just added.

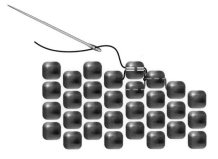

When you come back to the decreased edge, make a turn without adding a bead.

Shaping Within the Beadwork

These techniques are similar to making darts in fabric. Use them when you want your beadwork to expand or contract, such as when covering a curvy bottle or gourd.

Simple increase

Simply use two beads in place of one bead where you would like to increase. Choose two beads that are narrower than most.

Try to use narrow beads when adding two for an increase.

On the next row, add one bead between the two narrow beads.

Complete the increase in the next row by adding a normal sized bead between the two narrow beads.

Figure 2. On the next row, pass through the two narrow beads without adding a bead.

Double or gradual increase

This method provides a more gradual increase than the simple one. Use two narrow beads in the spot where you want to increase (Figure 1).

On the next row, pass through the two narrow beads (Figure 2).

On the next row, use two narrow beads in the same increase spot (Figure 3).

Finally, on the next row, add one bead between the two narrow beads (Figure 4).

Figure 3. On the next row, add two normal sized beads above the narrow beads.

Figure 1. For a gradual increase, begin by adding two narrow beads in the place of one.

Figure 4. Complete the increase by adding one bead between these two added beads.

Simple decrease

To decrease, simply run your needle through two "up" beads and pull them tightly together (Figure 1).

On the next row, add only one bead in place of those two (Figure 2).

Work the next row as usual. This step decreases the width of your work by two beads.

Figure 1. To begin a simple decrease, pass through two "up" beads without adding a bead between them.

Figure 2. On the next row, add one bead above these two beads.

Figure 3. Continue as usual, having decreased the width of your work by two beads.

Decreasing tubular peyote to a point

For amulet bags with a pointed bottom, fold an even tube flat, making sure that there is a "down" bead on each side seam, then decrease on each side seam by passing through two "up" beads. (When you're making the bottom point, turn your bag upside down and work *up* to the bottom.)

If you decrease at three or four equidistant points, you'll get a 3-dimensional triangular or square box shape.

To decrease to a point, pass through two "up" beads at each side "seam."

Double or gradual decrease

For a gradual decrease, pass through two "up" beads and pull them together (Figure 1, below).

On the next row, add two beads at the decrease spot (Figure 2, below).

On the next row, pass through the two beads added on the previous row (Figure 3, opposite).

Finally, decrease to one bead (Figure 4, opposite.

Figure 1. For a gradual decrease, begin as for a simple decrease, passing through two "up" beads without adding a bead between them.

Figure 2. On the next row, add two beads at the decrease spot.

Figure 3. On the next row, pass back through these two beads without adding a bead.

Figure 4. Complete the decrease by adding one bead above the two.

Making Geometric Shapes

You can use these shapes to embellish other beadwork, assemble them to create dangles, or combine them to make larger shapes.

Diamond

Start with about two feet of thread. Because you have to pass through the points of the diamond several times, use a single thread and beads with large holes. Tie a keeper bead about 2" from the end and string an odd number of beads (we used thirteen). Pass back through the

To begin, pass back through the fourth bead from the needle.

Vicki used circles and diamonds as beads in this whimsical necklace.

Photograph by Joe Coca.

fourth bead from your needle. The diamond is worked around the center row of beads, first above, then below.

Work peyote stitch across the row toward the tail. Add two beads at the end and pass through the very first bead heading away from the tail. You now have a sideways bead on each end.

After completing the third row, you will have a "sideways" bead at each end of the work.

Work peyote stitch back to the other end. Pass through the three beads on the end.

Work peyote stitch towards the tail. Pass through the end (sideways) bead. Remove the keeper bead and tie the needle and tail threads together in a square knot and pull tight. Trim off the tail thread to about ⅛", but don't glue it. You can leave the tail to weave in later, but it is much easier to control the tension while working if you tie it off now.

Pass through the next two beads. Peyote stitch around and around, passing through more end beads with each row until you have a complete diamond shape. Tie off your thread as usual.

Continue to work around, passing through the beads in the points without adding new beads.

Triangle

To begin, string on an odd number of beads. These will form the centerline of your triangle. The illustrations show a triangle started with thirteen beads.

When you return to the first end, pass through the three beads that comprise the point.

When you get back to the tail end of the diamond, remove the keeper bead and secure the tail thread.

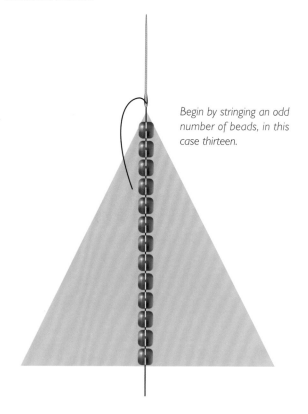

Begin by stringing an odd number of beads, in this case thirteen.

First we work one side of the triangle, then we do the other side. Work four rows of regular even-number peyote stitch (see page 23).

Work four rows of regular peyote stitch.

When you get to the end of the fourth row, add a bead, and go around the end to the other side. The last bead added becomes the top (point) of the triangle.

At the end of the fourth row, add a bead and pass through the "up" bead on the opposite side.

Work peyote stitch to the end of the row, making two steps down (passing through two beads as illustrated) at the bottom end of the triangle.

Make two steps down at the base of the triangle.

Add a bead and pass through the second and third beads from the end (making two steps up as illustrated). Work peyote stitch as usual toward the top of the triangle.

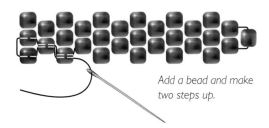

Add a bead and make two steps up.

You will not stitch all the way to the point of the triangle; the row will be completed when you've gone through the last "up" bead. Now you must turn and bead back toward the bottom. To change direction, you'll take what Jeannette calls the "ten-cent tour." After adding the last bead for the row, pass through the next two "down" beads. Turn and pass down through two more beads on the other side. Turn and pass through the middle bead, then turn and pass through the next two beads. You are now ready to head toward the bottom end of the triangle.

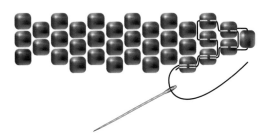

Weave the thread through the pointed end of the beadwork as shown, ending with the thread ready to head back toward the base of the triangle.

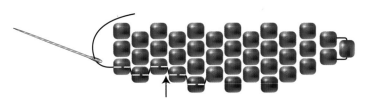

When you reach the base, make two steps down.

Peyote stitch as usual back toward the bottom. When you get to the end of the row, you will have to make *two* steps down before adding a bead and passing through the last "up" bead as illustrated.

Turn, add a bead, and pass through the first up bead as usual. Now add a bead and make two steps up.

Add a bead, make two steps up, and head back toward the point.

When you reach the last "up" bead toward the top, take another ten-cent tour, weaving through the beadwork as before, but without going all the way to the point, and ending so your thread comes back out of the last bead added and you are heading toward the bottom. Continue working up and down in this manner until this side of the triangle is complete, making two steps up and two steps down, and weaving through the work to change direction as necessary.

Now weave your thread through the beadwork to the top of the piece on the opposite side and complete the triangle. When you're working this second side, you don't have to make two steps down or two steps up, but you still have to take the ten-cent tour.

Chain Links

Links are simply strips of flat or circular peyote. Use a series of links to make a chain or dangle, use them to connect other geometric shapes, or use them alone to embellish other beadwork.

You can make "open" geometric shapes and link them together to make a chain.

Photograph by Melinda Holden.

Jeannette's Geometry Lariat *uses both solid shapes and chain links.*

Square and triangular links

Using doubled thread and tight tension for stiffness, make one- or two-inch peyote strips about one-quarter-inch wide; make four for each square, three for each triangle. You may make the strips either vertically or horizontally. The number of beads wide and rows deep will vary depending on the bead sizes. If your strips are floppy, sew through the beads again to stiffen them.

To create links, stitch the strips together, overlapping the ends. Sew the squares together at four points, the triangles at three. Remember to connect to the previous link before you stitch the last point of the current link together, like those paper chains you made when you were a kid.

Circular links

Begin as for tubular peyote (see page 29), but increase at random points around the circle so your beadwork will lie flat, like circular peyote. The end result is a circle with a hole in the middle. A one-inch ring is a good start for quarter-inch-wide beadwork.

You must start each link through the previous link before you join the beads of the current link into a circle. As you peyote-stitch around, rotate the bead loop to expose the area you are working on.

For square links, overlap the ends of four strips and stitch them together.

For triangular links, overlap the ends of three strips and stitch them together.

When making circular links, remember to begin each new link by working through the previous circle.

TipTipTip

When you've finished your links and they are still too floppy, dip them in Future Floor Wax (from the Johnson Wax Company). We learned this from beaders in Australia via NanC Meinhardt. We tried it and it works great!

Finishing Your Beadwork

Once you've completed your beadwork, take a good look at the finished piece. Are all threads neatly and securely tied off? If not, finish them by your chosen method, with or without knots (see pages 21 and 22).

Once all the loose threads have been taken care of, check for little fuzzies made by the thread. You may singe these off with a cigarette lighter or match (see page 18).

Check all fasteners (hooks, loops, buttons, etc.) and make sure they are securely attached. If you have any doubt, add more stitching to the questionable areas.

When you've finished a beadwork project, we recommend that you take the time to record it. Take a photo or scan it into your computer. Or take it to a copy shop and have a color photocopy made. Record the date you finished it, the name of the piece, and any special beads or techniques you used. If the piece is to be worn, put a few extra beads in a little zipper bag and set them aside for repairs. For an amulet necklace, we always put aside a bag with enough beads for an extra fringe as well as several beads for the strap.

If the work is for sale or for a gift, let us say that packaging counts! A small tag that bears the name and story of the work is a wonderful touch. Find or make a beautiful gift box to keep the piece snug and warm when not in use. And if the work is for sale, be sure and pay yourself well for your time. You deserve it!

Projects

Beaded Beads

Here are some of our favorite ways to make big beads out of little ones.

Rolled bead

One of the simplest things to make with peyote stitch is a rolled beaded bead. Just make a square or rectangle of flat peyote stitch, then bend it around until the up/down bead edges meet. The beads should fit together like zipper teeth. If they do not, simply bead one more row. To join the edges, pass your needle through the first up bead on one edge, then the first up bead on the other edge, and so on, back and forth until the seam is finished.

Rolled beads are a wonderful, quick way to experiment with color and pattern.

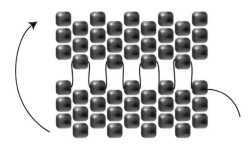

Bring two edges of a flat peyote-stitched piece together and seam them, forming a tube.

Rolled beads are featured in this necklace by Jeannette.

Tubular bead

Tubular beads are similar to rolled beads, except that the holes of the beads that comprise the tube go in the other direction. Here are instructions for an odd-number tubular bead with a two-color spiral.

String one light bead, two dark beads, two light beads, two dark beads, two light beads, two dark beads (eleven beads total). Now pass through all the beads again to form a circle. Pass back through one more bead on the ring and pull up tight. Tie the tail around the "core" thread or leave the tail hanging and weave it in later.

*String one (light) bead on your needle, skip one (dark) bead and pass through the next (dark) bead on the core thread. Repeat from * all the way around, always adding the same color bead as the bead you just exited.

From this point on, you will have "up" beads to go through. Add one bead to your needle, pass through the next "up" bead, again always adding the same color bead as the bead you just exited, until the tube is as long as you like. Tie off your thread.

Create a spiral of tubular peyote by alternating two colors of beads.

TipsTipsTips

Keep your work tight! Be sure to always work in the same direction. (If you're right-handed, you'll work from right to left.) If you want the spiral to go in the other direction, add the color bead you are going into rather than exiting. You may change the spiral's direction every few rows for a lightening bolt pattern.

Sculptural beaded bead

Choose a large wooden, Lucite, or plastic bead to cover with peyote stitch. You will cover this bead completely with smaller beads, so the color doesn't really matter. But if you're worried, choose a bead of similar color to your seed beads, or paint it if you like.

Use tubular peyote to create stand-alone beads or to cover existing tubular-shaped beads.

Photograph by Joe Coca.

Most of the charm of freeform sculptural peyote comes from the mixture of bead sizes. Mixing the sizes creates ripples and waves in your beadwork. Keep your thread tension tight as you work. Work in patches of color, rather than alternating single beads.

The sculptural or irregular surface of these beads is created by using small beads of different sizes and shapes.

Begin by tying the thread through the hole and around the bead (Figure 1).

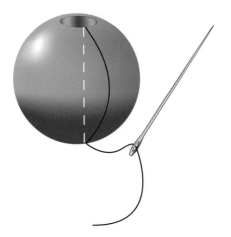

Figure 1. To begin covering a large bead, tie an anchor thread through the hole and around the bead.

Move the knot to the edge of the hole, then string enough beads to reach along the outside of the bead from one end of the hole to the other. The first strand of beads should be of varying sizes and shapes.

Go down through the hole of the big bead and tie the thread to the thread you tied around the big bead (Figure 2). Hold the big bead with your thumb and index finger, covering the hole to prevent the beaded strand from slipping inside the hole.

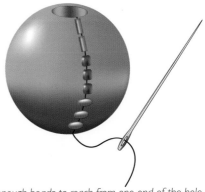

Figure 2. String enough beads to reach from one end of the hole to the other.

Now work peyote stitch to add a row to the strand of beads. To keep the colors continuous, add the same type of bead you are skipping—i.e. in Figure 3 on the next page, add red and skip red, add blue and skip blue, add blue and skip blue, add purple and skip purple.

Continue beading vertically for three to five rows. When you reach the center of your peyote-stitch area, add a row of beads horizontally around the big bead, connecting back into an up bead on the opposite side (Figure 4).

Figure 3. Form a second row by working along one side of the first strand.

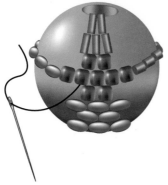

Figure 4. After working three to five rows, add a horizontal strand of beads.

Figure 5. Anchoring the horizontal strand in four places will help hold it in place while you work.

Work peyote stitch to add another row along this horizontal strand of beads. About every quarter of the way around, run your needle up through the hole in the big bead and back through the little bead your needle is coming out of (Figure 5). This secures the horizontal strand and keeps it from slipping around as you work.

Now here's where the real freeform begins. With your needle coming out of a small bead from the horizonal row just completed, string on enough beads to reach diagonally up (or down) and connect to a bead on a vertical row (Figure 6). Work a few rows of peyote stitch along this newly added strand.

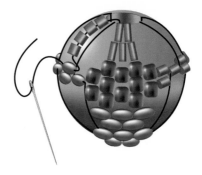

Figure 6. Create new vertical strands that run from the horizontal strand to the top bead of a previous vertical row.

Fill in the empty spaces by connecting to the horizontal, vertical, or diagonal rows as needed. Continue until the big bead is covered with small beads, adding more diagonal rows to work from as necessary. (See Figure 7.)

If your big bead has a small hole and you can't make too many passes through it, you can bead right over it. Just be sure you leave a little hole for stringing the bead when it's

Figure 7. Continue to create new rows and fill in between the rows until the entire large bead is covered.

Unlike the sculputral bead, these have a smooth surface because they are made with beads of the same size.

done. Put a tassel at the bottom and string the bead into a necklace of matching beads. Or try making a bunch of different-sized beaded beads and you can display a whole bowlful! They'll look great on the coffee table.

Peyote bead

This project uses beads of one size and or shape to produce a flat surface.

Tie your thread through the hole of your master bead and move the knot to its midline on the outside. String an even number of seed beads, enough to encircle the midline of your master bead. Go through all the beads again, plus one, to make a ring. Anchor this ring by going through the hole of your master bead, then through a small bead. Pass through a few more beads and anchor four to six times at equal distances around the ring.

Work a few rows of peyote stitch above the initial strand towards one end of the hole, then weave through the band and work below the initial strand for a few rows. This is even tubular peyote (see pages 29–30), so watch for those step-ups. Continue working around, first on the top half, then on the bottom, decreasing as you go. Use double or single decreasing according to the shape of the master bead and the size of your seed beads. For a regular pattern, you'll have to decrease at regular intervals. If your master bead shows through the peyote-stitched seed beads, you decreased too much. If the beads don't fit snugly against the master bead, you need to decrease more.

String a circle of beads along the midline of your large bead and anchor it in four to six places.

Jeannette's patchwork cuffs provide great opportunity for experimenting with combinations of colors and shapes.

Patchwork Collage Cuff

This cuff-style bracelet uses flat peyote-stitch techniques to make geometric shapes or patches.

First make twenty-five to forty flat peyote-stitch patches ranging in size from ½" × ½" to 1½" × 1½". You can make squares, rectangles, triangles, diamonds, and circles. Refer to pages 37–40 of the techniques section for instructions. Each piece should be made with one size, shape, and color of bead. It is best not to make patterns on your patches, because when you patch them together and embellish them, your cuff will look too busy.

After you've made most of the patches, arrange them as you intend for the cuff. Make more patches if necessary to make the cuff long enough to fit your wrist.

Patching the pieces together

Anchor your thread in one of the patches. Choose another patch and position it on top of your first piece at an interesting angle. Overlap it just enough that you can securely join the two patches. Pass through both patches with the needle and thread, stitching through a couple of beads then straight through both patches. Stitch through a couple of beads and through both patches again. Repeat until the patches are securely joined.

Join two patches by overlapping them and stitching through beads of both patches until they are securely linked.

Pass through beads until you reach the edge of one of the patches. Add another patch and repeat the process described above. Continue piecing the patches together at interesting angles until the cuff is long enough to fit around your wrist. It is okay to have open gaps between pieces.

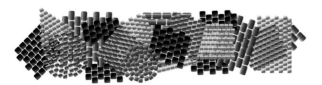

Continue to join patches at interesting angles until the piece is long enough to go around your wrist.

Embellishing the cuff

Embellish only the outside of your cuff. Add embellishments the same way you pieced the patches together, passing through beads in the embellishment and the cuff, and hiding your thread inside beads.

Embellishments can be large beads, wire shapes, or more shapes made from seed beads. Keep the embellishments close to the patches so your thread is hidden.

Triangle

Bring the needle up through the patch that you would like to embellish. Add six beads and pass back through the fifth bead, add five beads and pass back through the fourth, add four beads and pass through the first bead in the first strand of beads. Tack each corner of the triangle to the surface of the patch.

Zigzag

This is like the triangle only you don't join three sides. Continue to add five beads and pass back through the fourth until you have a zigzag that stretches across the patch you are embellishing. Tack each point to the patch.

Form a triangle, and end by passing back through the first bead.

Make a zigzag the same as the triangle, without joining the ends.

When the zigzag is long enough to fit your patch, tack it down at each end and at the points.

Circle

String on enough beads to make the desired size circle and pass back through the first bead in the strand. Tack the circle to the patch until it is securely joined and the circle holds its shape.

Make a circle embellishment by stringing on desired number of beads and passing back through the first bead.

Circles within circles

Make circles as described above, but make smaller circles to fit within these circles.

Decorate a patch with circles within circles.

Confetti

Bring the needle up through to the top of a patch. *Add a bead and pass back down through the patch. Pass through beads to another spot and come up to the surface. Add another bead and repeat from *. Continue adding one bead at a time until you have a "sprinkling of confetti."

Adding beads randomly creates a confetti effect.

Diagonal line

Tack a straight line of beads from one corner of a patch to the opposite corner at a diagonal. Pass back through beads in the patch to get to the places you want to tack the line to.

A diagonal line is easy to make. Be sure and tack it down in several places.

Rondelle

Rondelles are flat disk beads with a hole in the center. Bring your needle up through to the top of the patch. Pass through the rondelle, add one bead, and pass back down through the rondelle and the patch. That's it!

Use a small bead to hold a rondelle on to the surface of a patch.

Buttons with shanks make easy closures.

Wire shapes

If you know how to do wire work and want to add flat wire pieces to the cuff, simply stitch them onto the surface of the patch. You need to take only one stitch in three to five places on the wire to securely stitch it to the patch. Don't take too many stitches or you'll cover the wire with threads!

Tack a wire piece down only in as many places as necessary to avoid covering it with thread.

Finishing the cuff

Once you are happy with the surface embellishment, add a shank-style button and loop to the cuff. Stitch the button to the top surface of one edge of the cuff, passing back and forth through the shank as many times as you can for strength.

On the opposite end of the cuff, anchor a thread and come out a few beads from a corner. String beads on the thread and anchor the other end back into the cuff to form a loop. Check to be sure that the loop fits over the button before restitching through the loop beads as many times as possible for strength.

You can also use a long bead as a button, as in the cream-colored cuff. Notice that the two strands are joined with stitching to form one strand under the bead and create a shank. (See page 48.)

Wire hooks and eyes make great clasps, too. You can make your own to match the cuff, or check your local bead store for the perfect clasp, bead, or button for your cuff.

Create a loop of beads to fit over the shank button.

Peyote Flowers

Using circular peyote with increasing and zigzag-edge techniques, you can make these delicate little flowers to decorate an amulet pouch, a bracelet, or a vessel. Sew several to a barrette, or glue onto post backs for a dainty pair of earrings.

Use single thread, because you will have to pass through the outer beads several times. Start with about one yard of thread.

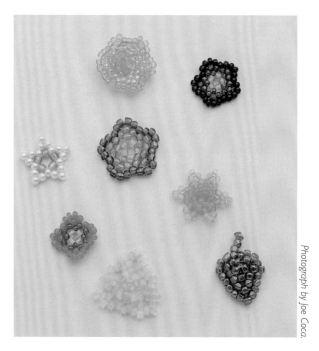

Photograph by Joe Coca.

Use flowers to embellish other items or to make earrings or pins.

Five-petaled flower

String five beads for your flower center. Pass your needle through the beads again, in the same direction, to form a ring. Pass through the next bead and pull up tight (Figure 1).

We will be doing even circular peyote, so remember to step up for each row by passing back through the first bead added in the previous row. Now begin to peyote stitch by adding one bead between each bead on the ring. (Figure 2. Add five beads total.)

Figure 1. Begin a flower with a five-bead center.

Figure 2. Add one bead between each bead of the center.

Add two beads between each "up" bead. (Figure 3. Add ten beads total.)

Figure 3. Increase by adding two beads between each "up" bead.

Add one bead between each "up" bead in the last row, in our illustration alternating red and purple. (Figure 4. Add 10 beads total.)

Add one red bead between each "up" bead. (Figure 5. Add ten beads total.)

Add two red beads, pass through three: the next "up" bead, one "down" bead, and one "up" bead. (Figure 6. Add ten beads total.)

Figure 4. Now add one bead between each set of two beads added in the previous row.

Figure 5. Work a normal row, adding one bead between each "up" bead.

Figure 6. Create an irregular edge by adding two beads, passing through three beads, adding two beads, etc.

If you like, you can sew a small button or bead to the center of the flower before tying off. Pass the thread through to get back to the center or add a bead to the center with the tail thread.

Variations

The number of beads in the flower center determines the number of petals. Varying the number of beads added between petals, and the number of beads the needle passes through at one time, will result in different petal shapes. Try starting with four beads, using shades of blue for a forget-me-not. Six beads in yellows with a tiny tubular center make a dainty daffodil.

Bead Pot with Drops

The inspiration for this tiny pot came from Mary Theresa Klotz's "Beaded Vessels" in the Fall 1996 issue of *Beadwork* magazine. It is made with size 11° seed, Delica, size 10° triangle, and drop beads. Techniques include circular peyote stitch, increasing, even-number tubular peyote, and decreasing.

Photograph by Joe Coca.

This little pot is made with four different types of beads.

Count out the beads for each row as you come to it. (The number of beads you will add appears in parentheses at the end of the row instructions.) Counting helps you know you've finished the row and are ready for the step up.

Begin with about three yards of thread, doubled and waxed. String five 11° seed beads. Leaving a tail to tie off later, pass through the beads. Pass through the first bead again to finish the row and step up. (Figure 1.)

Add one bead between each bead of the circle. Pass through the first bead added again to finish the row and step up. (Figure 2. Add five beads.)

Figure 1. Begin the pot with a circle of five beads.

Figure 2. At the end of the first row, make a step up by passing back through the first bead added in the current row.

Add two beads between each bead of the last row. Pass through the first bead added again to finish the row and step up. (Figure 3. Add ten beads.)

Figure 3. Add two beads between each bead of the last row.

Add one bead between each bead of the last row. Pass through the first bead added again to finish the row and step up. (Figure 4. Add ten beads.)

Figure 4. Add one bead between each of the two-bead sets added in the previous row. Step up to begin the next row.

*Add one seed bead, pass through one (seed) bead, then add one seed plus one Delica bead, pass through one (seed) bead. Repeat from * four more times. Pass through the first bead added again to finish the row and step up. (Figure 5. Add ten seed, five Delica

Figure 5. In this row you'll introduce Delica beads.

beads.)

*Add one seed bead, pass through two beads (one seed and one Delica), add one Delica bead, pass through one (seed) bead. Repeat from * four more times. Pass through the first bead added again to finish the row and step up. (Figure 6. Add five seed, five Delica beads.)

Figure 6. This row evens out with the addition of five seed and five Delica beads.

*Add two seed beads, pass through one bead (the second Delica), add two Delicas, pass through one (seed) bead. Repeat from * four more times. Pass through the first bead added again to finish the row and step up. (Figure 7. Add ten seed, ten Delica beads.)

Figure 7. Here we increase with both the seed and Delica beads.

*Add one seed bead, pass through one (seed) bead, add two seed beads (over two Delicas), pass through one (the last Delica) bead, add one Delica, pass through one (seed) bead. Repeat from * four more times. Pass through the first (seed) bead added again to finish the row and step up. (Figure 8. Add fifteen seed, five Delica beads.)

To make the beads spiral perfectly, make sure you put the two seeds over two Delica beads, and go into the fourth Delica bead.

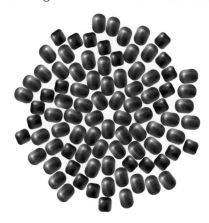

Figure 8. When working this row you add one seed, pass through one bead, add two seed beads (over two Delicas), pass through one bead, then add one Delica and pass through one bead.

Your circle of beads should be beginning to curl up into a bowl shape. Make sure that you keep your tension tight. *Add one seed, pass through two (seed) beads, add one 10° triangle bead, pass through one (Delica) bead, add one Delica bead, pass through one (seed) bead. Repeat from * four more times. Pass through the first bead added again to finish the row and step up. (Figure 9. Add five seed, five Delica, and five triangle beads.)

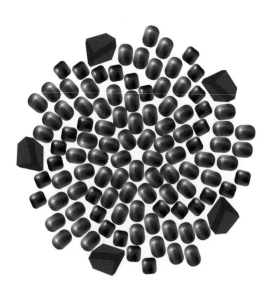

Figure 9. Once the piece begins to bowl up, we introduce triangle beads.

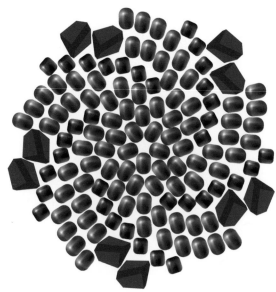

Figure 10. The bowl develops an interesting surface by using three different types of beads.

*Add two seed beads, pass through one (triangle) bead, add one triangle bead, pass through one (Delica) bead, add one Delica bead, pass through one (seed) bead. Repeat from * four more times. Pass through the first two beads added to finish the row and step up. (Figure 10. Add ten seed, five Delica, and five triangle beads.)

*Add two seed beads, pass through one (triangle) bead, add one triangle bead, pass through one (Delica) bead, add one Delica bead, pass through two (seed) beads. Repeat from * four more times. Pass through the first two beads added to finish the row and step up. (Figure 11. Add ten seed, five Delica, and five triangle beads.)

*Add one drop bead, pass through one (triangle) bead, add one triangle bead, pass

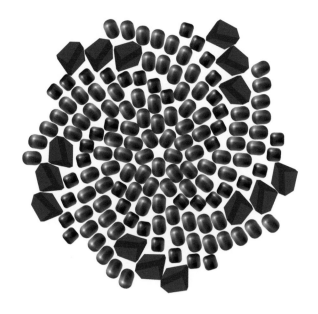

Figure 11. Step up through two beads at the end of this row.

through one (Delica) bead, add one Delica bead, pass through one (seed) bead, add one seed bead, pass through one (seed) bead. Repeat from * four more times. Pass back through the first bead added to finish the row and step up. (Figure 12. Add five seed, five Delica, five triangle, and five drop beads.)

Figure 12. Now add drop beads and repeat this row until the vessel is as tall as you like.

Repeat the last row until the vessel is as tall as you like. Remember to step up every row! If you want to close the top of your vessel, simply reverse the increase rows (leave out beads in the reverse order that you added them, pulling your thread very tight) until the opening is the desired size. If you keep decreasing until the top is closed, you'll have a marvelous beaded bead.

Tip

Watch carefully for tangled thread. Check at the end of each row to make sure the thread is pulled up tight.

Another Tip

Finish the current row before tying off the old thread. Then you may add new thread and come out of any drop to begin the next row.

Freeform Sculptural Peyote Bowl

This bowl is done freeform and requires good peyote-stitch skills. You'll need to use your own judgment in several instances to decide how many beads to add and in which spot.

Photograph by Jeff Tippett.

A freeform sculptural bowl, like this one by Jeannette, really lets you show off your peyote skills.

Because the bowl needs to be stiff to hold its shape, use a doubled thread. The bowl is also reinforced with extra stitching.

Begin by putting three beads on the thread then passing through them again (Figure 1). Leave a tail to tie off.

Pull the thread tight and the three beads will form a triangle (Figure 2).

Figure 1. String three beads and pass back through all three.

Figure 2. By pulling the thread up tight, the three beads will form a triangle.

Tie the threads together, glue the knot, and cut the tail thread. (Or you may pass through one more bead again to avoid making a knot. Then you can weave in the tail later.) Add one bead between each of the three beads (Figure 3). You may use the same size beads, or begin to add different sizes here.

Figure 3. You may begin adding different sized beads with the first row or wait for the second row.

Add beads between the outer three beads (Figure 4).

This is where you will need to use judgment when adding quantities of beads to fill in spaces. Put the beads on your needle, but don't move them down onto the thread yet. Hold them up to the gap you want to fill between the "up" beads. Do they fill the space? Add or subtract beads to get the right number to fill the gap without bulging or collapsing the piece. Once you have the right number of beads on the needle, pass through a bead. Try not to add more than two beads at a time, even if you have to pass through a "down" bead and an "up" bead before adding more beads. This keeps the work nice and stiff.

Figure 4. Add a row as usual, using different size beads.

Continue working around and around, keeping the beadwork flat by increasing as you go. You decide how large or small you want the bowl to be, but we suggest beginning with a small bowl until you get the feel of how to shape your piece. For a small bowl, the bottom should be about two inches across before you stop regular increasing.

If you gradually reduce the number of increases (rather than stopping altogether), and pull the thread very tightly as you stitch, you will notice the work beginning to pull up into a bowl shape. Regulate the increases so that the shape doesn't pull up too drastically and create a cup rather than a bowl. (Try a cup shape on another project. You may love it, too!) Continue beading around and around. Be sure to begin blending colors to prevent straight stripes. Put one bead of the previous row color on top of new colors as you go around.

You can add fancy embellishments, shells, semi-precious stone beads, wire shapes, small lampworked beads, or pressed glass beads as you go. When you're adding larger beads, use a few of the beads from the bowl palette to lead into and out of the larger bead. This technique will hide the thread as you span the gap up to the hole of the large bead (Figure 5).

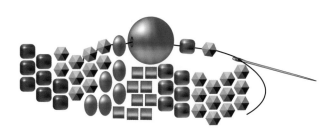

Figure 5. When your bowl progresses, add a large bead for embellishment if you like.

Bridges are a nice way to add texture to your bowl. Simply string a bunch of beads on your thread and attach to an "up" bead in the bowl. Make sure the beads arch up to look like a little bridge (Figure 6).

Continue to work peyote stitch around the edge of the bowl. When you reach the bridge, peyote stitch up and over it (Figure 7). Repeat

this until it becomes part of the structure. The top of the bowl will not have a flat or even edge.

Figure 6. The bridge technique leaves some open space in the vessel.

Figure 7. When you add more rows to the bridge it will become fully incorporated into the vessel.

All the techniques that follow for the sculptural pouch may be incorporated into a bowl. The only difference is that you must balance the weight of a bowl so it won't tip over. Experiment with different surface embellishment, and add anything to the structure you think will look good.

General Rule

Add the same type of bead that your thread is coming out of.

This freeform sculptural pouch is worked from the bottom up. The first few rows form the bottom, then you work around and around, creating a tube shape. There's no need to go back and seam the sides or bottom!

Photograph by Jeff Tippett.

Sculptural Peyote Pouch

This pouch is constructed from the bottom up, using odd tubular and sculptural peyote techniques.

Begin with an odd number of different sizes and colors of beads (Figure 1). Leave a two-inch space between the knot or keeper bead (see page 20) and the row of beads. Unlike other pouches, the beginning row will be the entire width of the pouch—we do not fold the row of beads in half with this technique.

The first row forms the bottom "seam" of the pouch, and you work along one side of this row, then turn and work along the opposite side. There is no need to go back and stitch the bottom closed.

Pass back through the second bead from the needle. (Do *not* add a bead here.) This step causes the last bead to turn on its side. You may need to help it along if it doesn't turn on its own (Figure 2).

Work in peyote stitch to the end of the row. You have a bead on the tail thread and add a bead to the needle thread (Figure 3).

Now cross over to the opposite side of the beadwork by putting your needle through the bead on the tail thread, essentially making a U turn with the thread (Figure 4).

Peyote-stitch along this edge to the end where the bead is turned sideways. Pass through that end bead, making another U turn so you will be on the opposite side again. Keep the tension tight as you bead along this side to the two-bead end.

Figure 1. Begin with an odd number of different size beads.

Add a bead, turn and pass through the "up" bead on the opposite side of the beadwork (Figure 5). When you tighten the thread, the new bead will sit on top of one of the two end beads. You are now beginning to form the sides of the pouch.

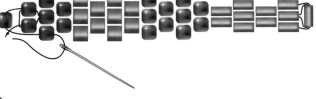

Figure 2. Pass back through the second bead from the needle.

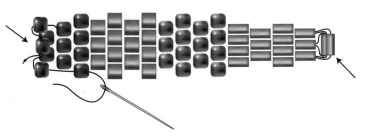

Figure 5. With this row, the sides of the pouch will begin to form.

Bead along the edge to complete the row, then cross over by adding a bead on top of the end (sideways) bead. The beads on the ends that are now stacking are indicated with arrows in Figure 6.

Peyote-stitch along the opposite edge as usual. When you get to the two-bead end, add a bead, go through the stacked bead, and cross back to the opposite side. Add a bead and go through the "up" bead as shown.

Figure 3. At then end of the row, when you have one bead on the tail thread, add a bead to the working thread.

Figure 4. Pass through the bead on the tail thread and come out on the opposite side of the work.

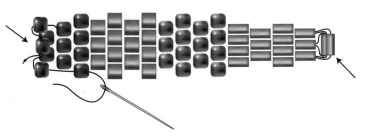

Figure 6. You will be working first one side, then the other in a circular fashion until the pouch is as tall as you like.

You should now be able to fold your bead-work into a little canoe shape. Fold and pull the thread tightly as you continue to bead around and around your little "canoe."

To prevent your beadwork from looking striped, blend one color into another. When blending, you may use two or more smaller beads to blend over a larger bead of the same or a similar color. This will also keep the thread from showing (Figure 7).

Figure 7. Putting smaller beads over a larger one prevents the thread from showing.

You are now working odd-number tubular peyote stitch. There is no need to "step up" for each new row—just continue beading around and around. Add fun little features such as bridges of beads and large novelty beads. Leave holes here and there and add wire shapes. Add any type of surface embellishment you wish. Like the bowl described on pages 57–59, the top edge will be very "sculptural."

Add a necklace strap to the top and fringe to the bottom if desired. The strap may be a long narrow peyote strip, a tubular rope, or a strand of beads reinforced by sewing back through the strand two or three times. Look in the gallery section for ideas for things to add to your fringe. You may use a different fancy

bead at the end of each fringe. Make each fringe a different length to keep the end beads from getting tangled. We recommend that you continue the colors from the bag down into the fringe so it looks like it belongs to the pouch.

To make a "double-run" fringe, exit from a bead on the bottom seam of the pouch and string all the fringe beads. Add one "anchor" bead. This can be one seed bead, a group of seed beads, or a fancy drop bead or charm. Now pass back through the fringe beads—make sure you skip the anchor bead, or all the beads will fall off! Pass through the next bead on the bottom "seam" of your pouch, and string the next fringe (Figure 8).

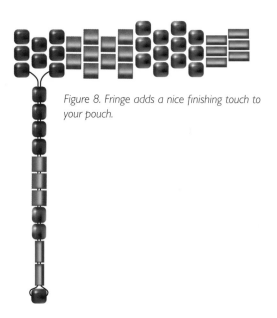

Figure 8. Fringe adds a nice finishing touch to your pouch.

Purple Mandala Amulet Pouch

Following a pattern

This little amulet pouch uses even tubular peyote and zigzag edge techniques. It has a straight bottom, and we work it from the bottom up in even tubular peyote stitch (see pages 29–30). It is constructed similarly to the sculptural pouch described above, but you will have a turning bead on each side and a two-bead step-up on every row.

When following a chart, remember that it is helpful to count out the beads for each row before you begin the row. This way, if you reach the end of the row and have an extra bead or two, or if you don't have enough beads counted out to complete the row, you'll know you've made a mistake and can correct it before you go too far to turn back.

To ensure that the pouch "fabric" is not too stiff, use a single thread and keep the tension a little loose as you work. Tie on a keeper bead (see page 20). String the first (and second) row beads, in order, from left to right. This will be an odd number of beads, and for this pattern we'll string on twenty-one blue beads.

Add the first bead of the third row, (a blue bead) and pass through the third bead from the needle, heading towards the tail.

Work peyote stitch back towards the tail by adding one blue bead, skipping one bead, and passing through the next bead. Repeat all the way to the next-to-last bead. Stop when you have one bead on your working thread and two beads left on the tail thread.

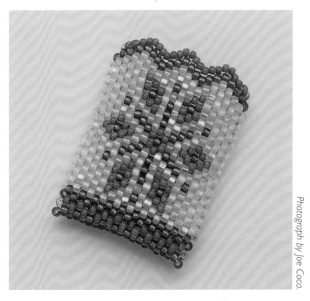

Work this amulet pouch to become familiar with following a chart.

Add a blue bead and pass back through the third bead from the needle.

When you finish the third row, you should have one bead on the working thread and two on the tail.

Things to Remember

Here are a few things to keep in mind when you're designing your own pattern for peyote stitch. You can make a straight vertical line, but horizontal lines are every other bead, or two or three rows staggered.

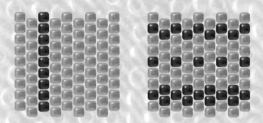

Straight diagonal lines only work at a particular angle.

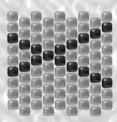

Circles and squares must be approximated.

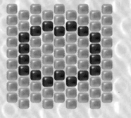 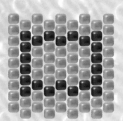

Those of you familiar with computer graphics already know that the more beads (or dots) per inch, the more detailed the design. The more complex the design, the smaller the bead or the larger the finished object. It's fun to just play with simple repeats to see what kind of patterns are possible.

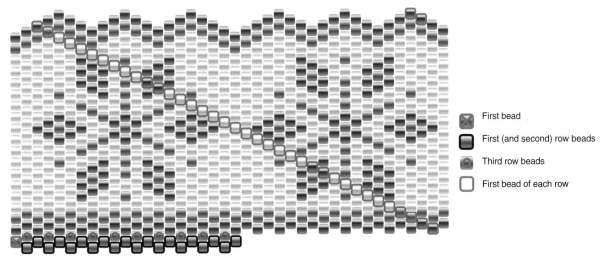

⊠	First bead
▢	First (and second) row beads
⊙	Third row beads
▢	First bead of each row

Mandala pouch chart.

Make a U turn at the corner by passing through the *last* bead on the tail, then through the next-to-last bead. This is your two-bead step-up at the end of the row. *Note:* The beads on either end should sit sideways.

Make a U turn and head for the other end of the pouch.

Work to the other end, adding one lavender bead between every up bead. When you get to the first corner, your added bead will sit on top of the sideways bead. This is the end of the first side of the pouch, but *not* the end of the row. Continue to peyote stitch around the corner and along the back side to the tail end.

When you get to the other corner, your added bead will once again sit on top of the sideways bead. These "top" beads create the side seams of your pouch. Pass through the "up" bead from the "first row" beads (a blue bead), then pass through the next (lavender) bead. This is the two-bead step up and you are *now* ready for the next row.

Once you've turned the corner, you're ready for the next row.

Work the pouch by doing peyote stitch around and around, following the pattern. To make it easy to keep your place in the pattern, place a ruler over the pattern and slide it up as you complete a row. Or you can make a copy of the pattern (for your own use, of course) and mark off the beads with a pencil as you go. Some beaders place their pattern in a plastic sleeve and mark off the rows with a wipe-off pen in case they make a mistake. Another alternative is to put the pattern on a piece of cardboard or foam board and stick a pin in the pattern to mark your position. Once you get used to following a pattern in peyote stitch, keeping track of your place is much easier. (But we still use the handy, dandy see-through ruler when we get lost! See page 18.)

For this pouch, the first three rows are blue. Then work two rows of lavender, twenty beads in each row. The next two rows are white, twenty beads in each row. Remember to step up at the end of each row. Now begin the motif as follows:

Next row: One white, one blue, one white, one lavender, five white, one lavender, one white, one blue, one white, one lavender, five white, one lavender. (Add twenty beads total, step up.)

Next row: Two white, one lavender, six white, one lavender, two white, one lavender, six white, one lavender. (Add twenty beads total, step up.)

Once you've worked these first two pattern rows, you will be able to see the design in your beads and the chart should be easy to follow. We are working even tubular peyote here, so remember to go through two beads at the end of each complete row (the last bead of the previous row and the first bead added in the current row). Notice that the two-bead step-up moves diagonally around

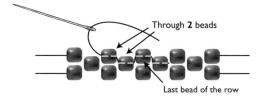

The step up at the end of each row will move over by one bead from the previous row.

the pouch, one bead over with each row.

Caution: When tying off and adding new thread, don't pull too tightly or your beadwork will wrinkle.

Continue following the pattern, and use the zigzag edge technique (see pages 31–33) when you get to the top. Add a simple neck strap, using doubled thread for strength. Do you like fringe? Then by all means, add some!

Photograph by Joe Coca.

Ice Princess *by Jeannette Cook.*

Gallery of Contemporary Peyote Stitch Beadwork

On the following pages you'll find some of our beadwork along with that of some of our beady friends, colleagues, and students. While these are but a few of the possibilities that beading with peyote stitch offers, we hope they will inspire you to get out your beads and create your own unique compositions.

Deep Space   5"W × 15"H.

Jeannette Cook. Lemon Grove, California.

Dragon Morgana   7¼"W × 3"H.

Jeannette Cook. Lemon Grove, California.

Traveling Stick   13"W × 4"H.

Photograph by Melinda Holden.

Photograph by Melinda Holden.

Peyote Bowl on Driftwood   8¼"W × 4½"H.

Jeannette Cook. Lemon Grove, California.

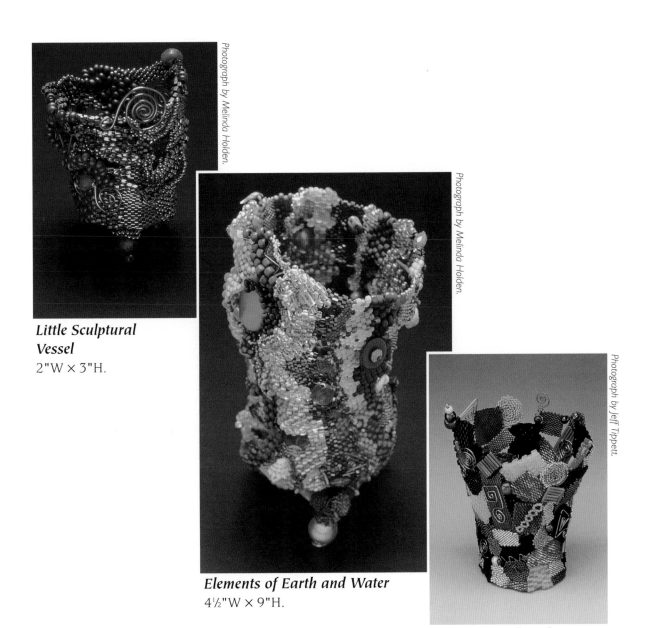

Photograph by Melinda Holden.

**Little Sculptural
Vessel**
2"W × 3"H.

Photograph by Melinda Holden.

Photograph by Jeff Tippett.

Elements of Earth and Water
4½"W × 9"H.

**Tapestry Patchwork
Collage Vessel**
4"W × 5½"H.

Jeannette Cook. Lemon Grove, California.

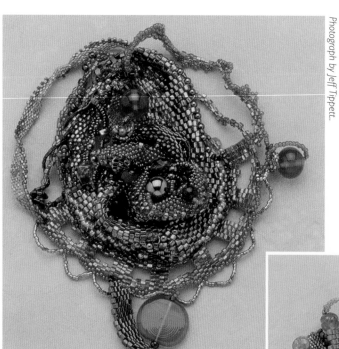

Journey in Beads   4½"W × 5¾"H.

Epic Cuff   7½"W × 3½"H.

Jeannette Cook. Lemon Grove, California.

Wedding Necklace   4"W × 14"H.

Photographs by Melinda Holden.

Aloha, Sarah   4½"W × 14"H.

Jeannette Cook. Lemon Grove, California.

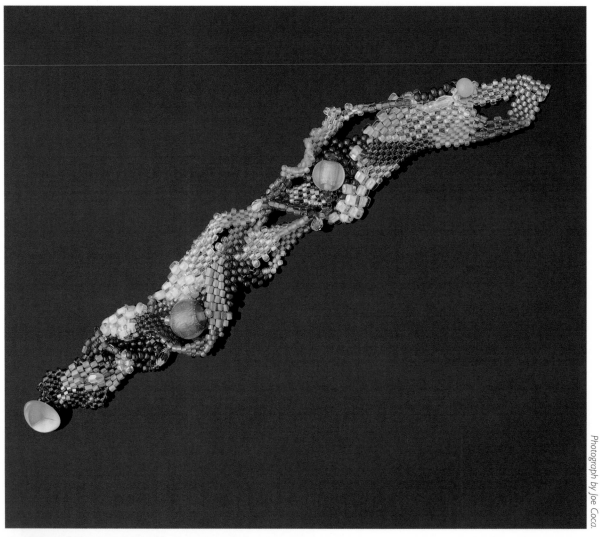

Photograph by Joe Coca.

Sculptural Peyote Bracelet   1"W × 7"L.

Vicki Star. Encinitas, California.

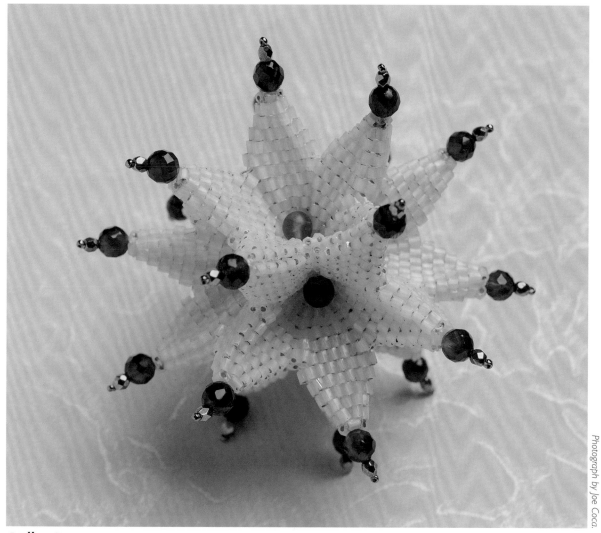

Stellar Star   3½" diameter.

Vicki Star. Encinitas, California.

Photograph by Joe Coca.

Amulet Pouches   Violet: ¾"W × 1"H plus fringe; Paisley: 1⅝"W × 2"H; Iris: 1"w × 1¼"H plus fringe. Various strap lengths.

Vicki Star. Encinitas, California.

Dragon Pouch   1½"W × 2"H, tail 5"L.

Vicki Star. Encinitas, California.

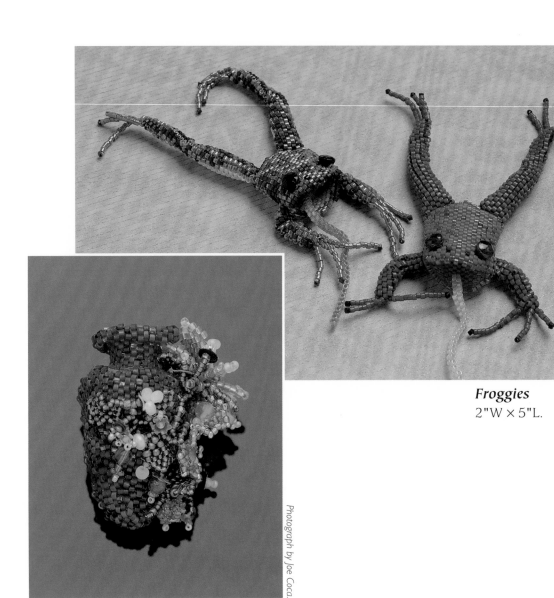

Froggies
2"W × 5"L.

Urn from Cynthia Rutledge's Class
1"W × 1¾"H.

Vicki Star. Encinitas, California.

Baby   14"W × 20"H, including tail.

Tery Baker. Winter Garden, Florida.

Serpentes 9¼"W × 9¼"H.

Carol Bauer. Olympia, Washington.

Sea Spirit 2   4"W × 4"H × 4"D.

JoAnn Baumann. Glencoe, Illinois.

Mountain Skink   ⅜"W × 7½"L.

Spring Bishop. Halfway, Oregon.

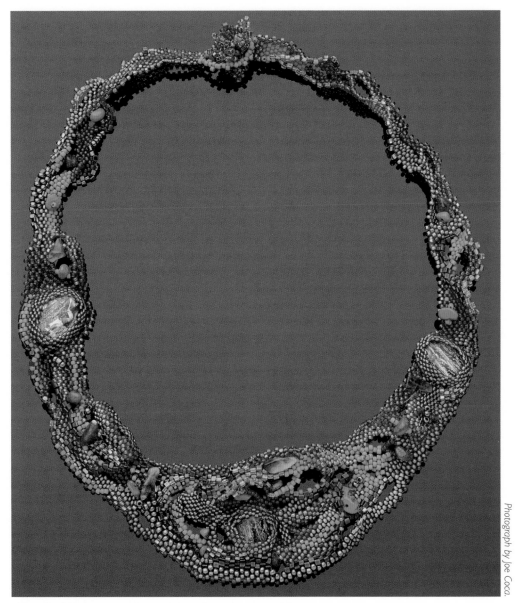

Mystic Mirage   8"W × 9"H, deepest part 2".

Karen Conolly. Azusa, California.

Opera Netting   2¼"W × 5¾"H, plus strap.

Dawn Dalto. Myrtle Beach, South Carolina.

Fan and Rattle in Size 18° Beads   Rattle: 1"W × 27"H;
Fan: 1" × 25"H.

David Dean. Galesburg, Illinois.

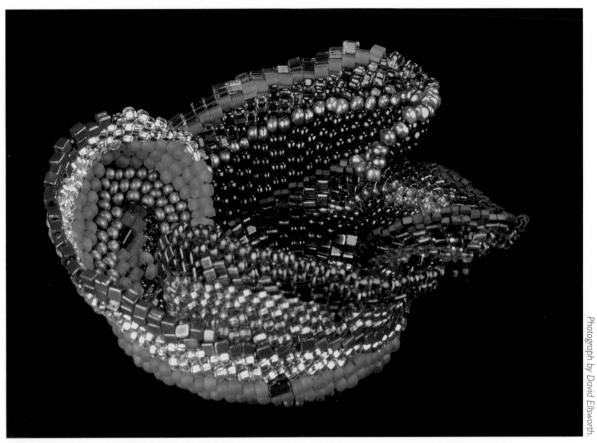

Spiral Galaxy   4½"W × 2½"H × 4½"D.

Wendy Ellsworth. Quakertown, Pennsylvania.

Photograph by Tom Van Eynde.

Butterfly 4¼"W × 3"H.

Leigh Everett. Brandon, Missouri.

Persian Stars   12"W × 16"H, panel 3¼"W × 8¼"L.

Diane Fitzgerald. Minneapolis, Minnesota.

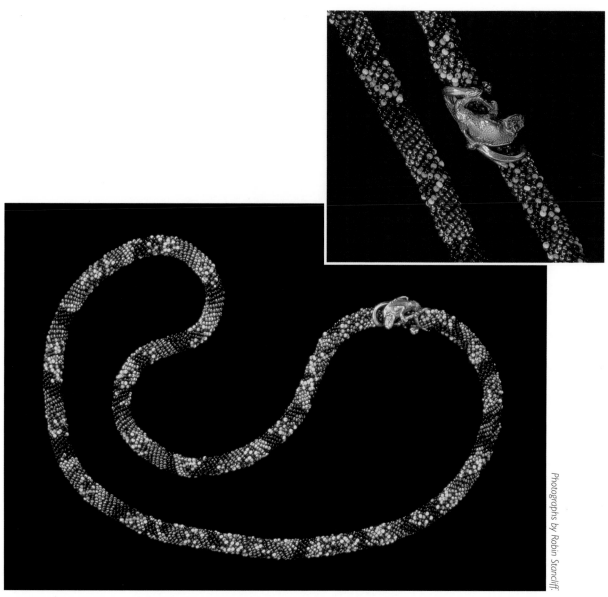

Photographs by Robin Stancliff

Iguana, Iguana   ⅜"W × 12"L.

Ann Fletcher. Tucson, Arizona.

A Garden for My Flowers   3½"W × 6"H.

Barbara Grainger. Oregon City, Oregon.

3" Earrings   ½"W × 3"H.

Barbara Judy. Franklin, Tennessee.

I Do 6½"W × 12"H. The fringe goes down the back.

Lisa Niven Kelly. Redwood City, California.

Untitled   1"W × 3¾"H.

Jolie Mann. San Diego, California.

Amulet Bag   3"W × 5½"H, plus strap.

NanC Meinhardt. Highland Park, Illinois.

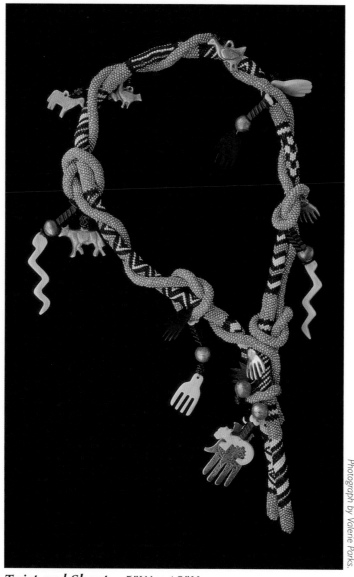

Photograph by Valerie Parks.

Twist and Shout   5"W × 19"H.

Kathy Mudge. Reno, Nevada

Green River Shaman   2"W × 5¾"H, plus strap.

Maxine Peretz Prange. St. Charles, Illinois.

Photograph by Joe Coca.

Wasp Necklace   7½"W × 8¼"H.

Kimberly Price. Toronto, Ontario.

Photograph by Roy Mullin.

Agnes   3"W × 8"H.

Susan Ridgway. Homer, Alaska.

Photograph by Ray McKee.

Desert Mooonrise   5"W × 13"H.

Kathie Schroeder. Tucson, Arizona.

3-Tiered Amulet Bag   2"W (Bar 4"W) × 7"H, plus strap.

Carol Small-Kaplan. Highland Park, Illinois.

Needlecase   ¾"W × 5½"H.

Lynn Smythe. Boynton Beach, Florida.

She Sells Sea Shells   15"H.

Tracy Stanley. Kirkland, Washington.

Photograph by Joe Coca.

Rainbow Bag   2½"W × 10"H, plus strap.

Judy Walker. Irvine, California.

Chinese Spirit Guide   3½"W × 7"H.

Rachel Weiss. Charleston, South Carolina.

Top: **Dragonfly Card Case**   4½"W × 2¾"H.
Bottom: **Salamander Card Case**   4½"W × 2¾"H.

Karen L. Whitney. La Mesa, California.

Endangered Garden   3"W × 5½"L, plus strap.

Judi Wood. West Palm Beach, Florida.

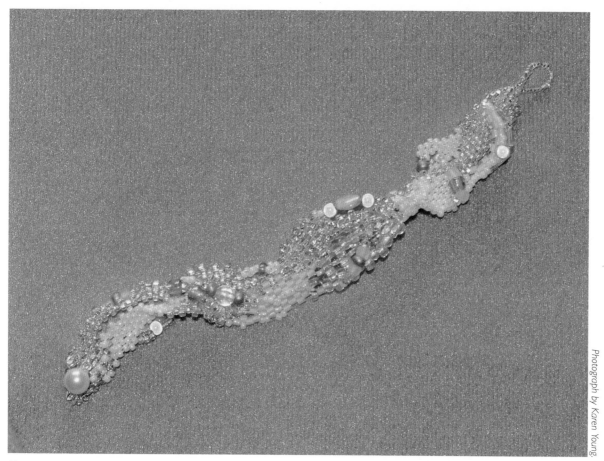

Frost   1"W × 7¼"L.

Karen Young. Tucson, Arizona.

Malignant Paradise
9¼"W × 7¼"H, including frame.

Nancy Zellers. Aurora, Colorado.

Photographs by Clark Mishler.

Where the Sea Meets the Shore   10"W × 11"H.

Penny Zobel. Anchorage, Alaska.

Bibliography

Aikman, Susanne Z. *A Primer: The Art of Native American Beadwork*. Denver, Colorado: Morning Flower Press, 1980.

Clabburn, Pamela. *Beadwork*. Haverfordwest, Great Britain: Shire Publications Ltd., 1980.

Dean, David. "Is it Peyote or Beadweaving?" *Beadwork* magazine, Volume 2, Number 3, Summer 1999.

Dubin, Lois Sherr. *The History of Beads*. New York: Harry N. Abrams, 1987.

Goodhue, Horace. *Indian Bead Weaving Patterns,* revised edition. St. Paul, Minnesota: Bead Craft, 1984.

White, Mary. *How To Do Beadwork*. New York: Dover Publications, 1972. Originally published by Doubleday, Page & Co., 1904.

Sources of Supply

Books, Kits, Patterns, Classes, and Beads
The Beady Eyed Women
PO Box 231093
Encinitas, CA 92023-1093
www.beadyeyedwomen.com
> *Beady Eyed Women's® Guides to Exquisite Beadwork:*
> *A Peyote Stitch Primer*
> *A Netting Primer*
> *A Bead & Weave Primer*
> *A Fringe & Edge, Tassel & Trim Primer*
> *A Sculptural Peyote Stitch Primer*
> *An Off-Loom Bead Weaving Primer*

Graph Paper
Beadcats
PO Box 2840
Wilsonville, OR 97070-2840
www.beadcats.com
> Send $2.00 for catalog

General Bead
317 National City Blvd.
National City, CA 91950
www.genbead.com

Graphing Software
Cochenille Design Studio
PO Box 4276
Encinitas, CA 92023
www.cochenille.com
> Stitch Painter for Macs and PCs

Gigagraphica
958 Vetch Circle
Lafayette, CO 80026
members.aol.com/equesse/gallery.html
> Beadscape for Macs

Practical Applied Logic, Inc.
The Virtual Bead Works
228 Dry Brook Rd.
Oswego, NY 13827-2813
beadville.com
> Bead Pattern Designer for PCs

Index

About Beadwork

BEADWORK magazine is devoted to every kind of bead stitching and creating. Its pages are filled with the latest innovations of the craft, including seed bead stitching, wirework, lampwork, and bead knitting, crochet, and embroidery. **BEADWORK** features beautiful photographs and drawings that illustrate projects designed by beadworkers all over the world. Its artist profiles, tips, calendar, and reviews allow readers to keep their fingers on the pulse of the international bead community.
$24 (6 issues) 800-340-7496.

Other Beadwork Books

The Beader's Companion
Judith Durant & Jean Campbell

Beader's Companion is a concise, user-friendly book that details beading techniques. It has sold over 16,000 copies.

7 × 5, spiral-bound, 112 pages, #671 —$19.95

Beading on a Loom
Don Pierce

Now in its second printing, *Beading on a Loom* is a comprehensive book that covers all aspects of contemporary and historic loomweaving.

8 ¹/₂ × 9 paperbound, 112 pages. #1027 — $21.95

The Best in Contemporary Beadwork
Coproduced by **BEADWORK** magazine and The Dairy Barn Cultural Arts Center

A beautifully designed art book containing work by leaders in the comtemporary beadwork movement.

9 × 11, hardbound, 144 pages, color photos. #1031 — $29.95

Coming in Fall 2000:

All Wired Up: *Wire Techniques for the Beadworker & Jewelry Maker*
Mark Lareau

8 ¹/₂ × 9, paperbound, 128 pages. #1029 — $21.95

**Call (800) 272-2193 or visit us online at www.interweave.com
to order your beading books!**